JENNY COOK

Cover design: Ultimate World Publishing
Layout and typesetting: Ultimate World Publishing
Editor: Emily Riches

Ultimate World Publishing
Diamond Creek,
Victoria Australia 3089
www.writeabook.com.au

What People Are Saying

"Jenny Cook has an enthusiasm for life that is irresistible.

I am lucky enough to know her professionally and personally and she is always the same Jenny; friendly, fun, and future-focused.

She has the ability to demonstrate what it is to truly live in the moment but always has an eye on what's next.

For her, that is very likely to be a trip overseas for work or pleasure, a new course she is doing or teaching to either learn a new skill or teach one, plans for the weekend, or the year, or the rest of her life.

Some of us who know her love the story of her going to her first yoga session and announcing her plans to teach it. Why not? A teacher is a teacher always and she has, over the course of her life, already taught dancing, aerobics, painting, personal development, and business as well as coached (mostly) women on how to design their own fabulous lives à la Jenny.

And yes, no surprise, she is now a yoga teacher among her very many talents and accomplishments.

Work with Jenny. She is amazing."

Dr Karen Conrad
Senior Lecturer
Curtin University

"In 2005, I decided to get back into the career world after years of being a stay-at-home Mum. I signed up to do a business course and that's where my life changed. I met Jen – she was my business trainer – we became friends and then travel buddies.

It's impossible to meet Jen and for your life not to change with her fun, bubbly, and adventurous personality.

I have never met someone with such zest for life. Her get-up-and-go attitude is infectious.

If I could be half the person she is, I would be happy. After spending a few hours with Jen, I always come away feeling inspired and wanting to do more with my life.

I have always been in awe of her ability to see life as a challenge, always stepping out of her comfort zone, so I was not surprised about her decision to take an adult Gap Year. I admire her for achieving all the amazing things she does, all the people she meets the places she visits and the experiences that only some can achieve.

Jen has definitely accomplished so much in her life and always with a smile. We all need a Jenny in our life; someone to inspire you to laugh with and to explore what life has to offer."

Emma Wilsmore
Former Student, now friend

About The Book

"Jen writes a captivating account of adventures that just makes me want to experience it for myself. How can you have all that fun and lose weight too? Take me with you next time, Jen!"

Tania Kelly
48-year-old, desperately seeking a gap year

"I seriously love it!

Makes me want to pull the plug immediately! Not bad for just one chapter! This book will change people's lives for sure. It is *Eat Pray Love* the second.

Congratulations for every part of doing this – the journey and the writing."

Dr Karen Conrad
Senior Lecturer in Public Relations
Curtin University

"That was so good! You took me back to Sri Lanka! So many awesome memories, I can't wait to read the whole book!"

Sarah Dare
Travel Buddy

"I found this to be a very inspiring read. Lots of fun and energy.

Having been to India myself and the areas mentioned, it made me want to go back again. Great memories.

It also inspired me to follow my dreams in life and grab every opportunity life gives you. Great read and well written. Felt as though I was part of the journey."

Di Hall
Travel Lover

"I wish I had this book with me when I travelled a year ago.

So many helpful tips and exciting adventures. It has inspired me not only to take another gap year, but just to have more fun and adventure in my life in general. It made me pause and reflect on what is really important in life.

Thank you for sharing your story with us Jenny. Reading it felt like sitting on the sofa with you eating cheese and drinking wine."

Christie Little
Avid Traveller

Dedication

To my ever loving and supportive husband, Rob who embraces most of my many whacky ideas. Thank you for listening to yourself and jumping into this adventure with me. It won't be the last! Definitely the start of a new life balance.

To my sons, Matthew and Ryan, who never doubted me and always support me with whatever "brilliant idea" I have at the time. Thanks, I love you both.

To my mum and dad, who have inspired me to live a full life and encouraged me to follow my heart.

To all my friends and family for your love and support.

Contents

Introduction

"With age, comes wisdom.
With travel, comes understanding."
– Sandra Lake

Usually, a Gap Year is something that young people take when they're fresh out of high school before they settle into their chosen careers. However, when my husband and I left school, we either studied further or got jobs; there was no Gap Year back then. While I do remember a select few that did travel, it wasn't on our radar at that time.

After raising the kids and watching them take their own Gap Years, we thought, why don't we? The kids had settled into adulthood and fully engaged in their own lives, while we were still in a suburban house with just the two of us and our fur babies. The house was way too big now and we wished to live near the beach.

One day, whilst walking along the beach, we had an idea: let's sell the house in the 'burbs and use our small holiday house as a base while we travel for a year! It sounded incredible, almost unbelievable; what? Travel for a whole year?

In Australia, we are encouraged to work to retiring age (67 years at this time), but no one mentions a mid-life break. Generationally, we are living longer than ever before, and the retirement age keeps creeping up, seemingly out of reach. Therefore, it seems ridiculous not to take time out to balance and reconnect with ourselves, our health, body, and mind.

For us, what was really important was to have a really long vacation – something we could only dream about while we ran our own business. We wanted to enjoy this one life while we were able, to regain our health and happiness before we burned out. Owning your business can be very rewarding but it can really cost you in other areas of your life at the same time. For us, it was the stress of trying to balance running a business and life. In the last few years, we had some personally challenging times, like the death of Rob's dad, the sudden death of a friend, and other emotional transitions in life, which were all taking their toll.

When we stopped and noticed what we were doing – going around in circles, doing the same old thing, paying the same old bills in the same old house, having the same short holidays – we knew we had to change things up and we were grateful for the opportunities that were presenting themselves. We discovered that we were still capable of adventures and excitement and not too old yet. You don't know what's around the corner or what you are capable of until you change things.

"The definition of insanity is doing the same thing over and over again and expecting different results."
– Albert Einstein

I remember when I booked the one-way tickets to Bali for three uninterrupted weeks of bliss, it was surreal. I couldn't believe we were actually embarking on this journey. We had a timeline! No room for second thoughts now.

It was a "must-do" self-care investment that would remain with us forever. We didn't know what we were coming back to career-wise, but were confident we would work it out when we returned. We knew we didn't want to come back to the same life patterns and imbalances.

This was, by no means, an impulsive decision. We had children, a business, a house, and two gorgeous bulldogs that all needed consideration.

My story is about *our* Gap Year – so whether or not you are planning a Gap Year of your own, or you just need to make a change in your life, we hope our stories inspire you to plan your next adventure and take action to live life now!

Chapter One

The Same Old Shit

> **"Don't let making a living prevent you
> from making a life."**
> — John Wooden,
> American basketball coach

Taking a career break or Gap Year is the new rite of passage that is ageless and genderless.

We were exhausted and knew we could actually take a "Gap Year" ourselves, but wondered what we would do. What would a Gap Year look like for us?

For Rob and I, we needed to stop and consider what we truly wanted our lives to look like. We wanted to write the next chapter while we were still able to.

Life's Too Short

My mum and dad are my driving force to live life to the fullest and travel. For the last 29 years, since mum died, I have been ensuring I get the most out of life. Sure, my parents had good lives; they were happy, had kids, and caravan holidays. Dad owned his own business. But in their generation, they left school at 14 and worked till they died, pretty much. They had two-week holidays at Christmas, and one week for each school holiday period during the year. Dad worked 12-hour days (at least), often six days a week. Mum fostered babies for 25 years. When she retired from fostering, and Dad sold the business to retire, they moved bayside, got sick, and passed; not quite what they had planned. It was heartbreaking.

More recently, things were getting harder in our lives when Rob's dad died and his mum got really sick. We were grieving whilst still being accountable for the business, which is incredibly hard when your responsibilities don't allow you time out to heal.

Another poignant moment was when my best friend Chrissy's husband, Geoff, died suddenly of a heart attack at the age of 53. It was surreal. It was devastatingly sad to watch my best friend and her family cope with that type of grief. This was a blatant reminder of how precious life is.

Even though we didn't know anyone who had ever entertained the idea of closing a business to travel and live their dream, no one ever questioned or judged what we were doing – it was quite the opposite. They were inspired by our change in direction and future adventures.

Rob had built the business, Brentwood Kitchens, over the last 30 years; it had been his heart and soul, his identity. But at some point, if it stops being your heart and soul, you have to listen to your intuition. The business had a good name, reputation, and a great history. It was a brand that was recognised locally and we were happy to store what we needed to and start a new showroom upon return.

We were witnessing people around us passing away from illness, heart attacks, and suffering mental illness, which was in the forefront of my mind when I suggested changing things up a bit.

The timing was right to go soon, before the grandchildren starting arriving, because we knew we didn't want to miss a moment of that.

Dreaming is Good, but Doing is Great

So, my advice in this early part of the book is to start to live life now. Take a look at your current situation and see what you want to change. Sometimes we're on such a busy hamster wheel of life, we don't realise how exhausted we are, until one day, we realise we can't walk up that hill, or that our life has become so unhealthy and sedentary as we drive through yet another fast food outlet just to satisfy our hunger pains.

ACTIONS

- Describe your typical day now and then write down what your dream day would look like. Analyse the differences.

  What strategies could you put into place to live your new "dream" life now?

- Create a vision board to keep you focused.

  Set aside an hour or two, and Google the things you love to do or the places you would love to go. You can even write a whole bucket list and start putting your dreams together.

  To help you, I have created an Adult Gap Year – Tool Box. You can access it here: https://jennycook.life/AdultGapYear_ToolBox. This will help you create your vision and plan for your own Gap Year.

  Once you have a vision board, the planning is easy. Dare to dream the dream – the possibilities are endless!

The Big Decision

"When your values are clear to you, making decisions becomes easier."
– Roy E. Disney

We talked about this idea of our own Gap Year endlessly over a few months, but not much to others, as we had other responsibilities to fulfil and plans to make before it was made public news. Once we had decided on it and had a rough timeline, we could put actions into place.

It was an extremely busy year as we moved to Philip Island, renovated our home, and continued operating the business. We finally stopped all work on 30th November, 2018. It took us two months to finalise most of the business logistics. The landlord was selling the factory which matched our timeline of vacating the factory by January. We sold machinery, vehicles, equipment, and many other items. If we came back, we were never going to manufacture again; we would only need equipment for an office and showroom and outsource the rest.

We were very glad when it came to early January and we could see the departure date just a few days away. The excitement was building and the surreal feeling of our dream adventure was upon us. It didn't take long to pack our bags; we only had a backpack and carry-on case and didn't care if we forgot anything.

Travel Because Money Returns, Time Doesn't

When we thought about leaving this daily grind for something fresh, travelling was a "no-brainer" for us.

We have travelled overseas a lot over the last 12 years, but never for an extended stay. This was definitely on our bucket list of things to do. If we ever discussed what to do next, it was always travel, probably to Asia's warm climate. We have been to Europe and America as well, but Asia was our favourite, especially the climate and value for money.

People often ask us; why did we go? What made us take this time out?

Our five main reasons:

1. To prevent burnout (or worse) and re-energise ourselves.
2. To get fit and healthy for our next life chapter.
3. Live life now, live the dream – take the opportunity now.
4. The timing was right – before grandchildren came along.
5. Life experiences, stories, adventures – we love to travel.

Feeling fit and healthy definitely has its rewards. As time went on, we became fitter and healthier by adopting new habits. Our minds had time to unravel and we learnt to relax.

ACTIONS

- Adopt self-care as a priority in life. Live in the present moment. Don't wait and get your check-ups later – get them done now. Keep on top of "life maintenance."

- Fill your cup first – filling our own cup first enables us to nurture others.

- Implement happiness by blocking out some time each day to do fun things. It's goal setting for a happier new you.

INITIAL HEALTH REPORT (January)

When we left, we felt unhealthy, bloated and tired from stress and over-indulgence from the festive season. Here are our initial stats.

Weigh In:

Jenny – 71.5 kg
Rob – 107 kg

Exercise:

~ The occasional walk ~
~ Yoga once a week ~
~ Meditation occasionally ~

Typical Food Intake:

Breakfast: A toasted sandwich or eggs on toast, coffee
Lunch: Ham and salad wrap
Snack: Coffee and whatever was quick
Dinner: Chicken parma with chips and salad, or pasta
Drinks: Water, tea, and plenty of wine and beer

Chapter Two

Chilling Out

"Investing in yourself is priceless."
– Jenny Cook

We had said goodbye to most of our family and friends before we left. To celebrate with them prior to leaving for a year, we had two Christmas days, our son Ryan's birthday, and a big New Year's Eve party.

Matt, my eldest son and his wife Britt (and their dog Pumba), had already moved in to look after the house and Ryan dropped us at the airport. By the time we were at the airport, we just wanted to get on the plane! Enough thinking and talking about this trip; let's just do it.

We arrived in Canggu, Bali, late at night, so we checked in and got some dinner at the hotel. To be finally there and to start our much-anticipated trip was awesome and a relief.

I had originally only bought us one-way tickets to Bali to create a timeline and ensure we would leave, however we had to buy onward tickets prior to leaving Australia as the Indonesian government won't allow you into the country otherwise. When we got to Bali, we had the first three weeks of total chill out bliss. There were no demands on us, there were no expectations. All we needed to do was get up, exercise daily, and eat wholesome food. Hard to take, huh? We looked at each other every single morning over breakfast and thought, "Wow, we're actually doing this thing. We are living our dream." We had stayed at Canggu many times and at this hotel, so we knew our bearings and just settled in for the duration.

We had come to get fit and eat properly, especially after the "silly season" of over-indulgence. On the first morning, we were up at 7 am to walk on the beach. We quickly realised it was hot at that time of morning and we would need to leave earlier to miss the heat. The next morning at 6 am, we set off again and were back in time for breakfast. I bought a Fitbit specially to monitor our steps and kilometres. We walked every morning on Canggu Beach; from Echo Beach area up to Finns Beach Club which was about a five-kilometre return trip. We also did a lot of other walking throughout the day, but our intention was for at least five kilometres. Then we got back home in time for breakfast, a swim, and yoga.

This was our morning ritual for the three weeks at Canggu. We would normally stay indoors or under the shade midday and afternoon, then head out for dinner in the evenings.

Then we added other activities. We'd swim, walk at lunch, go out for dinner, and at night, we would walk up to the band on Batu Bolong Beach. It's a beautiful walk along the beach at night, still around 26 degrees. Some days, we would easily walk ten kilometres.

Our food intake was so different to our normal diet, and we did this deliberately. The food is awesome in Canggu; it's easy to eat a fresh, balanced diet. One of the main changes was not allowing any snacking. We found eating three really good meals sustained us throughout the day so that we didn't even think to snack. We hydrated with plenty of bottled water instead. We would have at least three litres each per day and more when exercising.

Our food intake looked like this:

Breakfast: Muesli, fruit and yoghurt, coffee
Lunch: Nasi goreng with chicken
Snack: Tuna tartar
Dinner: Chicken and vegetables, salmon and salad, or a prawn Buddha bowl
Drinks: Water and tea

Along with the exercise and healthy meals, we limited our alcohol and coffee intake. This meant less alcohol, less coffee, and more water. We actually preferred water in the hot temperatures. The added bonus of less alcohol meant our budget lasted longer too!

Our usual indulgent holiday would include mid-afternoon happy hour drinks, dinner drinks, and evening drinks. But not this time. It was awesome, as we had far more energy. I found if we had a drink at lunchtime, I would need a nana nap in the afternoon. A waste of time and money!

During our morning walks, we saw many surfers out. It looked beautiful. Rob said, "We should go surfing, do you want to have a go?" I've never surfed really – only once when Rob pushed me on the board, so I'm not sure if that even counts. There were plenty of surf lessons available along the beach, so we booked one for the next day. It was my 55th birthday present; never too late to learn, huh? I had a great instructor, Adi. We sat on the beach for an initial instruction of what to expect in the water and then in we went. Rob can surf, so he had a more advanced surfing lesson. It was so much fun. I remember when Adi pushed me on a wave and I actually stood up, he started woohooing, but I fell off when I looked over at him. I was excited that I was up. It's quite exhausting though, with a lot of paddling, getting up, falling off, and repeating. The waves were great that day, but we never really saw many good surf days after that.

We went for dinner that night at one of my favourite restaurants. It's called Ji, a Japanese restaurant in an old Chinese temple in Bali. I love it. The food is traditional, with amazing dragon rolls, tempura prawns, and cocktails. From the second-floor terrace, you can see the surfers and the beautiful sunset. We have been there a few times on my birthday. It's a treat.

*****

We never hire cars in Asia, but we do hire scooters. As dangerous as that is, it gives us independence. Rob's been riding motorbikes since his early 20s, so he is an experienced rider. After the first eight years of me not even entertaining the idea of getting on the back of a scooter in Asia, it's now my first preference. We navigate around quickly, see things easier, we're more independent, and it's well worth our $6 a day to hire the scooter (including helmets).

However, you must have an international licence. About four days into our trip, we decided that we would go on a nice day trip on the scooter to Uluwatu from Canggu. It's quite the trip, as it takes about two hours on a scooter. However, we never found out because we didn't make it past Kerobokan. We stopped after hearing a whistle and saw two policemen waving their arms and pointing at us. Uh oh; we felt like rabbits in the headlights. Everyone else had stopped and we were at a standstill in this huge roundabout. We must have looked ridiculous.

"Red light, red light. Come, come, you must come," yelled one policeman. We pulled the bike over to their police station (a small shack on the side of the road) and were told, "Go in and sit." They both looked a little intimidating and kept saying, "Red light, red light, you no stop". They advised us that we needed to pay a fine of 500,000 rupiah (AUD $50) for allegedly going through a red light or end up at the Denpasar Court House tomorrow and pay more. We had heard of this type of fine but had never been pulled over before. Due to our stringent budget, we'd only taken 500,000 rupiah with us, and we were very quickly relieved of it.

Next, the policeman wanted to see Rob's international licence – otherwise, it would be an extra one million rupiah fine (AUD

$100). Rob assured him he had an international licence and began rummaging around in his backpack, reassuring them that, "It's here somewhere," meanwhile knowing full well he didn't have it with him. It was on the side table back at the room (lucky he didn't tell me that, or I would've been freaking out). However, the very kind policemen said not to worry, but to carry it with him in future.

Lesson learnt; Rob took that licence everywhere he went from then on, securely placed in a zip lock bag to preserve it. We were pulled over many times during our trip but never received another fine. We got off lightly, really.

After relieving us of our daily budget, the two policemen stopped traffic for us and gave us a police escort across the same busy highway to be on our way. So, it seemed we invested our money in a police escort. We never did make it to Uluwatu as we had very little money left, so we decided to ride to Sanur instead.

*****

I was heading off to India soon for a yoga retreat that I'd booked with my friend Sarah. Realising that India was cold in February, and all I had with me were summer clothes, I needed to go shopping (on a budget) to get something warmer. There are western-style shopping centres in Kuta and Seminyak, but they mostly had summer clothes and were more expensive than I wanted. After all, we were only into the second month of travel, so I wanted our finances to last.

I decided to go local. We passed some market-style shops on the scooter, so I got Rob to stop at one and bought colourful leggings, a black puffy jacket, and a striped red jacket. There were limited offerings and not particularly my taste or a fashion statement, but they did keep me warm for a total of AUD $22.

*****

Nusa Lembongan is a small island located southeast of Bali. It is part of a group of three islands that make up the Nusa Penida district. We had never been to these islands, so we booked the fast boat which takes around 35 minutes from Sanur. We had seen signs about the islands when we were at Sanur last time (the day we got booked by the policemen) and it looked beautiful. We booked tickets for the next day and were collected from our hotel in Canggu at 6 am to drive to Sanur. Rob booked a night's accommodation at Dream Beach Huts on Dream Beach. He did well! It was beautiful.

We left most of our stuff at the hotel in Canggu and just went on a quick adventure to Nusa Lembongan. The roads were very rocky and coarse on Lembongan. Getting to Dream Beach took about 20 minutes but the roads were so rough it seemed like more. The infinity pool was amazing, so we swam and had lunch by the pool. The huts were rather basic but nice and cosy with an outdoor bathroom. There were many of these grass huts scattered around the beautiful seaside gardens. We didn't really need to leave the resort; it was so beautiful. We loved it so much we took our friends Rhonda and Ian there later in the trip.

We booked a snorkelling trip from the hotel for the next morning. The little tuk-tuk took us to the other side of the island where we caught the long tail boat out through the reef.

We realised quickly that this wasn't an organised snorkelling trip, but rather a local and his boat who'd been hired to take us to the reef. The old wooden boat was a traditional fishing boat with outriggers that stabilised it; the paint was peeling off, showing its age and history. The driver spoke no English, which made it really interesting.

We rode in the boat for about 10-15 minutes, then the boat just stopped. We looked at the driver, who was now handing us snorkelling gear. We looked at each other and laughed. We thought, "Ok, we must be snorkelling here." We put on the masks, and with a lot of hand waving and pointing from the driver, we jumped in. Wow! He did know his snorkelling spots! The fish were amazing. It was a mass of colour and movement right there. There were so many different varieties of fish of different sizes and colours swimming by. We just floated while they swam around us. It was really breathtaking.

We stayed in the water for around 20 minutes, then the driver called us back with a whistle and we moved on to the next destination. This was much the same, with slightly different, larger fish. Then the third stop was unbelievable. The driver stopped near a cliff and he pointed to where we should swim to. As soon as we saw it, we knew instantly what he was trying to show us.

About 15 metres from the cliff was a complete drop in the ocean floor. The rock formations became like a "shelf," and the water was a deep blue/black colour, indicating its depth. The sun was streaming through the water making it more magical. It was a bit daunting looking at this massive drop where the water became infinitely deeper. Rob said, "It reminds me of the scene in 'Finding Nemo' (the movie) where the water gets deeper from the shelf and Nemo and the others were saved from the open water." After about 2 hours, we headed back to the beach and the driver picked us up there, as arranged. The snorkelling trip was a little daunting at first, as we didn't know where we were going, when we'd be back, or how to communicate with the driver, but it was an amazing experience.

*****

It took quite a while for us to start to unwind from the stress and get used to a longer stay. I looked at Rob during the first three weeks in Canggu, wondering, "What's he really thinking about? Is he finished with the work thing? Is he relaxing yet?" But I could see him physically starting to unwind. He started doing more, laughing more, and relaxing. I think he was in a state of shock for a while, just getting accustomed to not having to work and answer to anyone, which he's never really done in his adult life.

Many nights we walked to the band on the beach. Rob even went surfing one night during sunset. He said it was awesome, with the sun setting while he could hear the band from the beach. I sat on a beanbag near the band reading until he came in from surfing. It's truly amazing how little you need to spend to have an awesome time there.

Our "chill out" time was coming to an end. We were feeling great after just three weeks; lighter, more energetic, less lethargic, and ready to tackle the next adventure.

MY TOP TIPS FOR HIRING A SCOOTER

- You must have an international licence. Organise this from home before you leave.

- Generally, you need to leave your passport as security. If so, try and hire from your hotel as they will already have your passport. If you don't bring your passport, they may charge you a large holding deposit.

- Keep your international licence in a zip lock bag to preserve it.

- Ensure you take the key out of the scooter when parking it.

- Take a photo if parking in busy car parks to make it easier to find. There can be thousands of bikes in one area.

- Take photos of the scooter before you leave to identify any dents or scratches.

- Hire from your hotel or somewhere recommended to you.

- Always wear a helmet.

- Don't go through red lights!

HEALTH UPDATE – WEEK 4 (February)

We were feeling lighter already and doing more. Our mind and bodies were relaxing and we were definitely benefiting from less junk food, less alcohol, and more water. We both lost a little weight, but felt the benefits all over.

Weigh In:

Jenny – 70 kg   Lost 1.5 kg
Rob – 102 kg   Lost 5 kg

Exercise:

~ Walking 5-10 km daily ~   ~ yoga ~   ~ meditation ~
~ swimming ~

Typical Food Intake:

Breakfast: Omelette or muesli, coffee
Lunch: Sushi, chicken fried rice, fresh juice
Snack: Nuts and/or fresh fruit
Dinner: Prawns or chicken and vegetables
Drinks: Water, tea, and the occasional wine and beer

Chapter Three

Mayhem and Madness of India

"The voyage of discovery is not in seeking new
landscapes but in having new eyes."
– Marcel Proust

Jenny's Off to India

I went to India for ten days in February, immediately after our
first three weeks in Canggu. I had already booked a six-day
yoga retreat in Rishikesh and was to meet my friend Sarah
there. When we booked our flights, we had decided to meet
at the stopover in Singapore before we got to Delhi. It was
great to catch up and ensured we'd find each other in Delhi
airport, as I was a little unsure if I would find her otherwise.
Meanwhile, Rob decided to fly over to his favourite place,
Patong Beach in Phuket, Thailand.

Our Initial India Experience

Neither Sarah or I had been to India before, so we weren't prepared for how much mayhem there was. We found out quickly though! We had booked a five-star four-day tour that included Delhi, Jaipur, and Agra before we met the group for the retreat. On our first day, we began with a tour around the main tourist sights in Delhi. This included a cyclo ride which is a cart you sit in while the rider cycles you around, like a rickshaw. The tour was a great way to acclimatise to the culture and mayhem of India. It was all the hustle, bustle, and colour I had expected. The streets were very populated and busy. The poverty of old Delhi and the outskirts probably stood out the most to me, far more than what I have seen in other Asian countries I have travelled to. It was dreadful, but the people still seemed happy and family-oriented.

Sarah's face and knuckles went white as the driver navigated his way through the tiny side streets of old Delhi with millimetres to spare on either side of the cyclo. I've experienced similar rides before, so I know it's quite frightening when it's your first time, but Sarah hated it! She just wanted to get off and go home, but we had no idea where we were. It was mayhem and nothing I said reassured her, so I did what any good friend would do – got out my phone and took photos of her plight!

However, as time went by, she got more comfortable and started to relax; by day five in Rishikesh, she had settled in so much that she was hanging out of the tuk-tuk for photos and loving it. As the adventure continued, she got even more comfortable; in fact, by day seven she loved it so much she wanted to live there permanently!

Mrs Cook is Royalty in India

One night during our three-night tour, we decided to go into a very fancy hotel restaurant, as it looked lovely and the menu read well. Sparkling wine is expensive all over Asia, so it was quite an indulgence to enjoy a bottle of wine, particularly in that hotel. This indulgence, in fact, cost us an extra AUD $80 – more than the same bottle of wine would have cost in Australia.

We were sitting at a beautiful, elegant table, when the head waiter came over to introduce himself as Aadesh. It seemed he was our private waiter, never far from our table to ensure that we were enjoying our meal and our experience at the restaurant. Aadesh continuously topped up my glass and wanted to ensure I was happy with the service. "If I can help you with anything at all, Mrs Cook, even if it's not on the menu, I can call on my head chef to prepare something especially for you," he said. Sarah's face was priceless. Whenever Sarah and I go out, she is normally treated like royalty; by that, I mean she gets pampered or receives VIP treatment. So, this night caught her off guard as it was all about Mrs Jenny Cook. I was so uncomfortable that I went red with embarrassment but Sarah laughed at me and said, "Well, what about me? Am I invisible?' We still laugh about this today.

The Taj Mahal

The Taj Mahal was definitely on my bucket list, so the day we set off to visit it was a big deal for me. We had two tour guides that explained each area of the mausoleum and took photos of us. There were thousands of other people roaming the grounds and the buildings as well, but that's to be expected at these very popular tourist attractions. Even with the crowds, it was truly breathtaking!

The Taj Mahal is an ivory-white marble mausoleum built by Mughal Emperor Shah Hahan in memory of his darling wife, Mumtaz Begum. Built in Agra, it is India's most famous monument and one of the New 7 Wonders of the World. And now I had been there! What an amazing moment; it was as exciting as I had anticipated. I nearly hyperventilated. I felt very blessed to tick The Taj Mahal off my bucket list.

We then visited carpet, rug, and fabric shops that were bursting at the seams with colour and texture. In one of the huge multi-storey buildings, we were treated to a glass of wine while we watched an amazing array of rugs and carpets appear in front of us. It was so theatrical with the handlers rolling out the magic carpets in a flurry of movement, gestures, and colour. It was quite the performance, rolling out the rugs to finish just at our feet, so they could not be ignored. The rugs were truly exquisite, expensive, and could be delivered to your home.

In another factory, we dabbled with fabric stamping, creating gems of our own as keepsakes. We stamped elephants onto fabric squares, which felt like a childhood excursion, but was fun all the same. From there, we moved into the fabric shop.

This was truly a sight. The fabrics were everywhere, displayed on the walls, in cabinets, and waved around by the several salesmen. Beautiful dresses, sarongs, and scarves in all colours and fabrics made for a spectacular sight and made me want to bring it all home with me. I did buy a very colourful traditional-looking turban as a keepsake.

The Yoga Retreat in Rishikesh

Our hotel for the retreat was right on the banks of the River Ganges in Rishikesh. Sarah and I shared a room with a river view. Rishikesh is located at the foothills of the Himalayas in northern India; it's known as the "Gateway to the Garhwal Himalayas" and the "yoga capital of the world." It is also known as the pilgrimage town and regarded as one of the holiest places for Hindus. Because of the religious significance of the place, non-vegetarian food and alcohol are strictly prohibited. It appeared we were on a detox!

The River Ganges was a sight to see, particularly in the mornings from our yoga shala, as the sun rose and produced pink hues and mist. It provided the most spectacular views during and after our morning meditation. What a way to start the day!

The more we did the meditation and breathing techniques, the easier it became. You felt fresh and revitalised afterwards. I found it easier to meditate in the morning as my brain was not yet clogged or busy from the day's events.

The river is one of the most sacred rivers to Hindus and flows through Rishikesh, where it leaves the Shivalik Hills in the Himalayas and flows into the plains of northern India. Despite the pollution further down the river, the water in Rishikesh is relatively unaffected, very clear, and very cold. The major polluting points are downriver in the neighbouring state of Uttar Pradesh.

We were fortunate enough to engage in many Hindu ceremonies during our retreat. On our first day, we had an Aarti ceremony at the private Ghat (a beautiful room or hut built right on the river, that has a platform and stairs into the water). In Hindi, Ghat means "river landing stairs" or "mountain pass," which was true in both cases.

The Aarti is one of the most important and popular ceremonies of the Hindu faith. It's often called the "ceremony of light," and involves lighting wicks and waving them to infuse the flames with the Deities' love, energy, and blessings. The lit wicks are passed around the group to allow members to receive the blessings infused within the flames. The term Aarti also refers to the prayer sung in praise of the Deity while the wicks are waved. It is sung joyously and fills the whole Ghat with vibration. It is one of the most incredible experiences I've had; it made me quite emotional. It was nearly overwhelming; to just witness the incredible gratitude and faith of the Hindus is very calming.

The retreat went for six days and was a compelling experience. The yoga was aligned with the Hindu philosophy and each day our practise was in tune with a different Deity. We visited the ashram that The Beatles attended in the 60s to write songs and saw the tiny rooms they stayed in. There was also an awesome café named after The Beatles in Rishikesh. It had great views, awesome food and Beatles memorabilia all over the walls – quite the experience.

We did a lot of breathing techniques during our yoga and meditation sessions. I loved these. We did practises which involved "cleansing" of things that no longer served us, using breathing, chanting, and actions to help relieve us of the "old" and allow room for the "new" prana or life force. I was trying to meditate my way to feeling safe around monkeys but it didn't really work (they still make me anxious).

Spiritually, I know I grew during this trip, and couldn't wait to see how the rest of the year would eventuate.

Shopping in Rishikesh was great too. Sarah and I were in a frenzy in one shop; I think we were there for a couple of hours and bought all kinds of unnecessary brightly coloured items, including clothing and jewellery. We also noticed that there were many cows wandering the streets in Rishikesh, as they are holy and worshipped by Hindus in India. The cow is considered a sacred animal, as it provides life-sustaining milk and is seen as a maternal figure, a caretaker of her people.

In India, we were open to learning new things about ourselves, cultures, and religions, and were happy to engage in celebrations of Hinduism.

We both had an astrology reading whilst there, which was really interesting. The reader needs your birth date, time, and place to interpret your chart. Previously, I never got involved in astrology or zodiac signs, as I was never really convinced that what was said was directed to me but was usually a generalisation about incidents that may or may not occur.

However, when I had my chart interpreted from only these three pieces of information – which could have been similar to many people born in the same hospital at the same time – I was open to the interpretation of my astrological houses. When you have your own birth chart read by someone that knows how to read the chart, as well as interpret and synthesise each piece of information, it can be a little overwhelming.

The planets, signs, and houses all play a part in reading your life. This man nearly blew me away! I went in with an open mind (still a poker face though) and didn't say much, to hear him out, and get a laugh. Well, the laugh was on me when he mentioned how many children I had, their gender, how many times I had been married (twice), my income streams, and some personality traits. I couldn't believe it.

The one thing that had me truly amazed was when he said that, according to my sun and moon, "You have high expenditure at the moment because you are travelling and not working until around September or October, but you will be ok." I thought, seriously, how could he know that!

Sarah had a similar experience with her reading and was quite amazed.

Monkeys on the Loose

Monkeys are everywhere in Asia. I don't really like them (that's probably an understatement). They look feral to me, probably because they are always picking nits off each other, and you hear many true stories of incidents and hospitalisations. The other reason is that their bites and scratches can give you rabies. We did have our vaccinations for rabies but I was still nervous, as we would need to get home for treatment if we got bitten, and I wouldn't be happy if I had to cut our dream trip short because of monkeys.

During the yoga retreat in Rishikesh, our group was out shopping and exploring when we needed to cross the river on a footbridge. It was narrow and monkeys sat on a steel ledge around our head height. We were told not to make eye contact or smile as they think that's aggressive. We walked quickly across the bridge, heads down, glasses off (they pinch them), hoping they wouldn't notice us. One of the men in our group previously got scratched by a monkey on that bridge and had to go to hospital. Luckily, his wife was a nurse and knew what to ask for and could inject it. This just made me more nervous.

We had to walk back across this bridge and the monkeys were going feral because a man had taken bananas onto the bridge to feed them. An eye roll to that man – what was he thinking? His little son was freaking out too. Sarah was ahead with another friend and left me well behind (thanks for that)! So, I thought I would just stick right behind two of the other girls from our group (I think I held her bag strap) to make it off the bridge safely. When we were off, they turned to me and stared. It was only then that I realised they weren't with our group at all – total strangers!

Once the retreat was over, a few of us flew out as a group, stopping at Singapore and then going our separate ways; Sarah went back to Melbourne, and I met Rob back in Bali. A wonderful experience in India was had.

Rob's Adventures

Rob flew over to Phuket for ten days while I was in India. He loves Patong Beach and the surrounding areas, so was excited to go back and enrol in some Muay Thai boxing classes at the gym in Patong. He found cheap accommodation near the gym and began some boxing classes. He was amazed at first by how exhausting they were, but loved learning new skills and getting fit at the same time. We would speak when we could, and he said, "It's great here, but a bit weird without you." We have always travelled to Phuket together, but he settled in by going to gym, exploring on the scooter, and playing pool at the small local bars.

Back Together Again

We both met back in Canggu at Joe's homestay at Echo Beach to decide "what to do next." We met Joe years ago when we went to his restaurant and he was talking about his homestay and pool, tucked in behind his restaurant. He's a lovely Balinese man who lived and worked in Australia for around 20 years, then came back to settle in Canggu about 10 years ago. It must have changed a lot since he moved back, as even we had noticed how much Canggu had changed in the last four years. His wife, Mary, and daughter are happy and kind people too. We drop in to see them like old friends when we are in Canggu.

Rob got sick on his last day in Thailand and slept a few days away in Canggu. When he was feeling up to it, we went up to Ubud for a few days and stayed in a homestay just off

Hanuman Street. He still had stomach cramps and a fever so we got it checked out. A stomach infection was diagnosed by a pharmacist. He got medication and recovered over the next week.

This was the first time we had stayed in a homestay. We had enquired at a few to find out what they were like. The homestay was lovely, as were the sisters that ran it. Wayan and Nyoman (typical Balinese names) were really helpful and it felt like family very quickly. I still stay there when I go to Ubud.

A homestay, as the name suggests, is someone's home, usually housing the extended family, including children, parents, and grandparents. If you haven't seen a traditional-style Balinese homestay, it's a bit like a compound of outside rooms. Some homestays have added purposeful guest accommodation, like this one, but the home starts off with a common area, usually without walls and raised from the ground, then a few other separate rooms for bedrooms and a kitchen. Most of their daily living is done outdoors in the common areas. They often have family celebrations in these common rooms and some houses have their own temples where they place daily offerings. Usually, the homestays are fenced off with high brick walls. This one had 12 guest rooms, a pool, and beautiful gardens.

While Rob was sick, I wandered over to the Yoga Barn, which is a beautiful holistic wellness complex with a huge array of yoga classes on offer every day, amongst other therapies. It is a really blissful retreat centre, including onsite accommodation, the Garden Kafe with a fabulous healthy menu (stocked by their own organic farm), and many yoga shalas. It is well known amongst yogis and tourists. I had never been, so I took the opportunity to go to a few classes and soak up the environment. It was truly blissful.

I also wandered up to the local Ubud markets, stopped for coffee, and read by the pool. I was still meditating daily, a routine I had kept up since the yoga retreat. I did this most days during the entire trip.

*****

When Rob was feeling better, we hired a scooter and rode up to Tegenungan Waterfall, which was truly beautiful, with a bamboo river crossing and a rope swing. It was crowded and there was a local wedding there; the 20-metre waterfall created a stunning backdrop. After I had swung on the big swing using the waterfall for photos, we wandered back on our scooter.

We also had a favourite coffee shop, A.R.A.K. Coffee, on the other side of Ubud, which we went to daily. It felt like home. We ordered coffees and just chilled there.

Rob doesn't like Ubud much and we both prefer the beach, so after about five days, we booked online to go and check out Legian. This turned out to be a mistake! It was so busy with people and markets, and was also really hot. I booked the IBIS hotel as it was cheaper than where we normally stay, so was worth a visit.

Upon check-in, we noticed a lot of older people there in big groups. We guessed that they all booked from Australia and came on a group discount. They hogged breakfast time in the restaurant, as well as the poolside deckchairs and the pool. It was like the movie "Cocoon" (1985), where a retirement home swimming pool becomes full of alien cocoons whose "life force" rejuvenates the elderly residents. Funnily enough, they treated *us* like the aliens. They didn't speak to us much and sneered at us when we splashed or dared to use the pool. Needless to say, we spent a lot of time on the beach away from the hotel, which is much more our style anyway. It was weird and sort of funny. But never again!

TOP TIPS ON IMMUNISATIONS

1. Check with your doctor on what immunisations you will need for your trip; this is dependent on where you are travelling to and the duration.

2. Prior to leaving, allow a few months to have all the required immunisations, as some need two or three doses.

3. Have rabies shots if you are going to remote areas for an extended visit and/or will be around dogs or monkeys.

4. It's a good idea to keep a copy of what immunisations you have had in case you end up sick or in hospital.

MONKEY BUSINESS

1. Hang on to your bag and belongings if you want to keep them – monkeys steal things when looking for food.

2. Don't carry food with you near monkeys, especially bananas – it will cause a frenzy.

3. Don't smile or expose your teeth to monkeys as it is threatening to them.

4. Don't make eye contact with monkeys – they can feel threatened.

HEALTH UPDATE – WEEK 8 (March)

The routine of more exercise, better food, less snacking, and less alcohol became increasingly easier. It's amazing what a difference that can make.

Rob was running daily and I was doing yoga regularly and could feel my strength and flexibility increasing. I was losing weight; I could feel it. My clothes weren't as tight.

We were benefiting just from relaxing together too. All the supressed stresses were starting to fade and we were mindful of doing lots of yoga and meditation. Rob was feeling far more at ease; even his face looked relaxed.

Weigh In:

Jenny – 67.5 kg   Lost 4 kg | Rob – 97 kg   Lost 10 kg

Exercise:

~ Walking 5-10 km daily ~   ~ yoga ~   ~ meditation ~
~ swimming ~   ~ running ~

Typical Food Intake:

Breakfast: Eggs, noodles, omelette, coffee
Lunch: Sushi, chicken fried rice, or vegetable curry, fresh juice
Snack: Nuts and/or fresh fruit
Dinner: Prawns or chicken and vegetables
Drinks: Water and tea, occasional wine or beer

Chapter Four

Rupees, Bengals, and Beauty

"I want to keep learning, keep exploring, keep doing more."
– Jessye Norman

Nyepi in Bali

We were still in Bali when the six-day celebrations of Isakayarsa, Saka New Year, began.

Nyepi is a Balinese "Day of Silence" which is commemorated every Saka New Year (usually in March). It is a Hindu celebration renowned in Bali. Nyepi means "to keep silent" and falls on the third day of the celebrations, after the dark moon of the equinox when day and night are of approximately equal duration.

The entire island comes to a standstill with no scheduled incoming or outgoing flights from Denpasar Airport. Hotels are asked to cover their windows, and all shops are closed. No light or candle will be lit in any Balinese home, and there will be no cars on the road, no motorbikes, and no people.

It's quite amazing to be in Bali during this time. You are not allowed out of your accommodation. Nobody is on the streets, nothing is open. During the other celebration days, the locals have many parades up and down the streets, and they spend months preparing for Nyepi.

There are varying rituals during these six days. One that stands out to me is Bhuta Yajna Ritual and Ogoh Ogoh Parade, which are performed one day before Nyepi, in order to vanquish negative elements and create a balance with God, mankind, and nature. The locals build, carry, and display Ogoh Ogoh statues that are up to 25 feet tall and very heavy. They carry them on bamboo grids around the streets in parades, with music. Locals and tourists come out to enjoy the parades.

The whole celebrations are festive and something you don't see anywhere else. The Balinese love it and are very happy to explain in detail what each day holds. Previously, we got caught out not having any supplies for Nyepi as we didn't realise we would be confined to the hotel. We were locked in our hotel with a limited food menu and no lights. We met a lot of people by the pool though.

I love being involved and learning from other cultures and religions. Understanding how other cultures engage in the world heightens our personal growth. It's interesting to understand their viewpoint, their beliefs, and what drives them. I also believe if we enter their countries, we are responsible for how we behave and should have respect for their beliefs and cultures. We have seen a lot of tourists behaving in a manner that is not appropriate in other countries, disrespecting cultural celebrations, holy temples, and the people. We left just before Nyepi this time.

We finished up our week by walking our 5 km and enjoying the beach and the local cafes. It was still quite hot, approximately 32 degrees every day.

In the meantime, our health transformation was going really well. We had been away for eight weeks now and we could both feel we were getting fitter. I kept a journal of our food intake, exercise, and measurements, to keep us on track. We were both on the way to feeling fabulous. We were still walking 5 km on the beach most mornings, and averaging 10 kms a day. Rob was getting fitter and started jogging every second day. We needed to buy him new clothes as he was shrinking out of his old ones already.

Home

I had booked a week home over the Labour Day weekend in March, so we headed back to the airport to fly home. I already had this planned as we needed to finalise some business and see the family.

Our son Ryan picked us up from the airport, which is quite a trip – about five hours return – but gave us a great chance to catch up. We had a lovely time catching up with everyone, but the best news was that we were going to be grandparents! Yay!

Next Stop – Sri Lanka

We were excited as we'd never been to Sri Lanka before and had heard how beautiful it was. Lonely Planet called it the number one place to visit in 2019, and we hadn't ever stayed in one place for a whole month while travelling.

We started at Unawatuna which had been recommended by a Facebook group with advice about Sri Lanka. I had booked one week here on the beach. I thought it was a good start. We landed late at night due to a delayed flight from our Singapore stopover.

When we finally got to our accommodation at 11:30 pm, it was deserted. There was no one in sight. The driver helped us find someone to let us in by knocking on the shopfront door downstairs. Sure enough, someone was sleeping in there and could let us into our room. In the morning we could see the beach from our balcony; it was a nice view. The beach was beautiful, the restaurants had colourful tables and chairs set out, and it looked very festive and welcoming. It was still very quiet. The beach was lined with beautiful palm trees, reminding me of Gilligan's Island; that rustic, unspoilt beauty.

We walked by a tourist office every day called GG Happy Tours, and eventually stopped in to have a chat with GG. He was a lovely Sri Lankan man, full of great ideas.

We booked a trip with him to see more of the coast and then to explore some popular tourist sights inland on the island. We would go from Unawatuna up the east coast to Weligama, Tangalle, Arugam Bay, Pasikuda, and Nilaveli, then on to the city of Kandy, and finally catch the train into the mountains of Ella to climb the famous Adam's Peak. We would be accompanied by a driver, Presad. We FaceTimed our friends Mark and Sarah from Unawatuna to tell them that we were off exploring, and they decided all of a sudden that they were going to come and join in on the fun. They would meet us in Kandy in a couple of weeks. How exciting!

We were very excited to see the Dares and explore with them. They became known as our adventure buddies.

Getting My Stitches Out

When we popped home in March, I needed to have a freckle cut out near my left elbow that the doctor was concerned about. I didn't want to leave it for the whole year, so he cut it out and got it tested. Thankfully, it wasn't harmful. However, the six stitches were still in my arm when we needed to leave as the wound hadn't healed yet. My doctor in Australia suggested that we go to a medical centre in Sri Lanka and get the stitches out there. A lot of our doctors in Australia are Sri Lankan, so I felt comfortable doing that.

A week later, when we were in Unawatuna, we found a medical centre to get my stitches out. The staff and doctor were all lovely and very family-based. The clinic was very rustic and dusty, in an old building. They had dust masks hanging from the ceiling with more dust in them than outside of them, but they had their utensils in solution. The doctor's mum came in with a child on her hip and two small children, then somebody else came in and suddenly we had the whole family in the room with us, chit-chatting and investigating my wound and getting in the photos. It was funny because we couldn't understand a thing they were saying. But they loved it.

I also had an infected blister on my left foot from the rubber thongs. It was looking red and sore, so the doctor checked this also. She said not to go into the seawater, as it wasn't that clean and would only aggravate the sore. After she cleaned it, she wrapped a huge bandage around my foot. It was hilarious because it looked like I'd been in a scooter accident or something similar. A dose of antibiotics and a different pair of shoes and I was good to go.

When we came out of the building, our scooter had been moved to underneath the shade, which was a lovely gesture and an added service! It was an interesting experience, and made me less nervous about visiting a clinic overseas (if it's ever needed in the future).

*****

So, we began our month of exploring Sri Lanka, starting south at Unawatuna for a week. We spent hours walking through jungle tracks in the area. It was beautiful, quite rustic, unspoilt, and not so touristy. There were hidden beaches with old boats pulled up to the rocks, local vendors selling fresh coconuts, and old sun lounges. We found a gem called Jungle Beach, about an hour's walk from our beach. It was quite stunning and quiet, and we stopped to enjoy fresh coconuts. They were delicious.

We walked around a lot every day exploring Unawatuna, and Rob even started jogging daily here to keep fit. There were many yoga studios to choose from and I think we tried most of them. We had a favourite one though with a gorgeous white dome-shaped shala made of brick. Ada was the yoga instructor and he had the most amazing voice when chanting mantras; it would vibrate all through the small shala and you could feel the energy. Rob had never really engaged in this type of yoga and he was loving it, doing all sorts of asanas and, on occasion, even chanting. Go Rob!

One morning, we decided to go exploring on the scooter along the insanely busy highway in Unawatuna. Their local transport is a red bus, and these drivers were mad! They moved for no one. I'm sure one bus missed us by inches as he hurled past going at an insane speed. Clearly, these buses were on a very tight timeline, or they found it amusing to scare the heck out of tourists on scooters. The sheer terror we felt when we saw a horrid red bus made us stop until it passed. It was the safest way.

Apart from the buses, it was a nice ride along the beautiful coastline. Palm trees lined the coast and glimpses of crystal-clear blue water were enough to make us to stop for a look. We stopped at Kalabama Beach for breakfast one morning. It was rather quiet there, very unspoilt, and beautiful. We sat in a restaurant on the beach and had a Sri Lankan breakfast, which is quite different to a western-style breakfast. We had sweet rice parcels, savoury string hoppers (a local dish, a bit like noodles served on a vine leaf), and a Sri Lankan omelette. The local food is great but very different to ours. There were plenty of surfboards out ready to hire, but it was the tail end of the surf season, so no one was surfing there. We kept riding up the coast, stopping in at other incredible beaches.

Throughout our trip up the east coast – stopping at Weligama, Tangalle, Arugam Bay, Pasikuda, and Nilaveli – the beaches just kept getting more rustic and unspoilt. It was a really incredible coastline that was fairly deserted at that time of year. It was so much like Gilligan's Island, with the coastline covered in palm trees and other coastal vegetation, and no high-rise buildings. The cover image for this book was taken at our last beach stop, Nilaveli Beach.

*****

Now that we knew our itinerary, we were booking accommodation for the next few towns ahead. Mostly, our accommodation choices were great and good value but on occasion we got it wrong. We booked accommodation online for Tangalle before we left Unawatuna. It looked like fun, it was cheap, and not far from the beach; a small log cabin that looked rustic and relaxed. What could go wrong?

When we finally found this place, the Coco Palm Villas, it was definitely rustic. It looked like a treehouse with a creaky little stairway to get to the balcony where our room was. Not a solid start. When we walked up the creaky stairs, the room was bare minimum; small and with a toilet housed in the room. A small closet-type area had a bamboo blind for a door, which, when rolled up, exposed the toilet; right there, in the centre of the room. The hand basin was right next to Rob's pillow, which looked hilarious. I took a video and posted it on Instagram, which got a lot of funny feedback.

We were totally fine spending our days and nights together in confined spaces, but this was pushing the limits of privacy. In fact, there wasn't any privacy in this "tree house" style accommodation. And we had even booked the superior room!

All I could do was laugh. Sometimes, online photos aren't necessarily accurate. There was no glass in the window. The door was lockable, but you could put your hand in through the window area and unlock it. There was no security of any sort; no safe, and the window looked a bit like a jail cell with bamboo sticks. There were two wobbly chairs sitting on the balcony.

This place was hilarious, but I hated it. I tell you, we can spend time together, but it was a bit too "up close and personal," even for us. Never again! While we managed to look for and find alternative accommodation, after much deliberation we decided to save our money and stay one more night. We had already paid, after all – but two nights was my limit. We saved our extra night for the next destination. It was funny though, and made for a good story (and video).

We headed off to Arugam Bay one day early, as we had stayed long enough in the "tree house" town.

*****

On our way up the coast, our tour driver Presad knew we wanted to stop for brunch, so he pulled into a local road-side restaurant. It was an open-air venue, a bit like a food court, in that you looked at the different styles of food, ordered, paid, then collected your food and found a table and chairs to eat at.

The food was very local, as were the people; there was no English at all out here. We had no idea what we were doing or how to order food, so after five minutes of trying to communicate and order brunch with no luck, we got Presad to help us.

We finally settled on string hoppers and a cup of local tea. In total it was 120 rupees, approximately AUD $1.20 for both of us. It was an interesting and fun stop – after all, we did want to experience being "local."

Elephant Spotting in Sri Lanka

We stayed at Big Blue Resort in Arugam Bay where we met and befriended resort owner, Bille. Bille was a local, young, entrepreneurial type, full of charisma and stories from when he was a tour guide. We wanted to see elephants in their own environment, not at the safaris where we had read that the safari utes rounded up the elephants for the tourists to take photos, which seemed unnecessary to us. We had decided we didn't want to support that kind of business. So, we asked Bille where, and if, we could find "free-range" elephants. He was so convincing and enigmatic that we totally believed we would see them in the wild just a 30-minute scooter ride from the hotel. He sat and explained where to find them and drew up a map explaining all the sights along the way. He was so engaging that we didn't doubt him or his hand-drawn map of where to spot roaming elephants.

We rode for miles and miles into what seemed like the wilderness to spot these massive animals in their own habitat. We got off the scooter and walked through rough dirt tracks leading to the waterholes, but there was nothing to see. There was evidence they had been there though, as we spotted elephant poo along the tracks. We did sight a few elephants on the side of the road, which was exciting and we stopped to take photos, but we wanted to see herds of them by the waterways as was promised by Bille and his map.

Alas, there were no herds of elephants. However, there were numerous other animals and reptiles, sometimes too close for my liking. A two-metre-long black snake was stretched out across the dirt track, sunning itself. Rob slowed down and, at the sight of it, I was ready to turn back. Rob decided to try beeping and it slithered across the track into the grass to make way for our crossing. Then, looking into the waterways and creeks, we saw crocodiles. That was it, I was out! Enough of the discovery tour please – take me back and get me a wine.

Bille couldn't believe his map didn't work and we didn't see herds of elephants. "Must be the wrong time of day," he said, "go a bit later tomorrow." Believe it or not, we went back the next day as we were determined to see the wild elephants. Again, no sightings.

*****

At Big Blue Resort, the monkeys were literally all over the place. They were quite big and grey, swinging from the banana trees right above our hammock, on the balconies, everywhere. They apparently did a weekly circuit of the area, eating all the bananas and causing havoc, to return a week later. They were a bit funny to watch when they tried to land on the brick fence and fell clean over the other side. We sat and watched them for a while, until they got too close. They are quite destructive in the resorts though; the word "pest" describes them well.

We're still not sure why, but we had a change of tour driver from Arugam Bay to the end of our trip in Ella. Presad was no longer with us; our new driver was Tuan. He was equally as nice and I think he had a better grasp of the English language.

We enjoyed the tour up the coast. Tuan would drop us at the next destination, advise us of what we were doing there according to the itinerary, and then he would pick us up to move on. Sometimes, he would stay at the same accommodation, as they had "driver" rooms, or would come for lunch with us. It was great to know that he wasn't far away, as the further we ventured up the coast the more isolated and local it got. I remember when we were quite far up the east coast at Nilaveli Beach, where the locals are Tamils; people with Indian origins that are descended from workers sent from south India to Sri Lanka in the 19th and 20th centuries. Tamils are the largest ethnic group in the Eastern Province and a minority in other provinces. They seemed nice enough, but didn't speak any English, so we felt a little isolated. They loved getting selfies with Rob though. He was a huge hit with the locals.

Tuan was with us one night, walking along the beach, when he explained his fear of the beach was due to his very sad experience during the tsunami that hit several countries on Boxing Day in 2004. He was still a child and lost family members and had to start his life again in another country. Meeting people like Tuan is part of why we love to travel; to meet and understand others who we would normally not meet at home.

Asian Beach Dogs

All over Asia, we saw so many beach dogs. They were out of control in certain areas. Most areas in Bali also had a large amount of beach dogs. They tended to get territorial and fight, and I didn't like that.

When we were at Weligama, walking along the beach, a cute but annoying young beach dog started befriending and following us. We realised, after a while, that he was using us as decoys to get along the beach. As soon as we approached another territory, the top dogs would appear from nowhere and try to stop the young one from coming with us. He caused so many fights that morning that we ended up going back to the hotel after trying so many times to get away from him. It must have looked funny, us running and hiding from a small dog, but it really ruined the serenity of our morning beach walk.

When we went further up the coast to Nilaveli Beach, there weren't many tourists. We were sitting at a beach restaurant in the sand and there were puppies everywhere. They were very cute. Asian beach dogs have a particular look. They look a little bit like a dingo crossed with a kelpie, I think. But like all puppies, they are adorable.

The problem was, we counted 18 puppies hiding in this one beach restaurant alone. There were so many places that the mums and pups could hide, under day beds, under the beach chairs, the dining tables. It was horrendous to think that in six months all those puppies would be grown up and causing havoc begging for scraps in the restaurant. They needed to sort out a plan for beach dogs, I believe, some sort of free community service where the beach dogs get spayed or de-sexed to alleviate the neglect and potential danger of fighting dogs.

The beach dogs were in abundance in Bali too, mainly Canggu and Ubud.

Sharks – Pigeon Island

Whilst we were staying at Nilaveli, we decided to go over to Pigeon Island by boat and snorkel for the day. Here, we came across one challenge we didn't even know existed. While we were snorkelling on one side of the small island, we got in the water only to realise there were three enormous sharks swimming around.

I was really nervous when I first saw them and nearly panicked, but when I looked around, I saw that nobody else was panicking. That meant these sharks weren't aggressive. They were just minding their own business and enjoying the shallows, obviously used to the tourists, but there was no warning that there was sharks around. It's a little overwhelming to see three sharks just cruising underneath you. It was an amazing adventure though, and I'm glad we did it (and survived to tell the story).

Lion Rock

Amongst the many sights we saw in Sri Lanka was Lion Rock. This massive rock juts out from a green tropical forest, deep in the middle of the country, in Sigiriya. This amazing rock formation is famous for the palace ruins at its peak, surrounded by the remains of an extensive network of gardens, reservoirs, and other structures. The rock itself is a lava plug left over from an ancient, long-extinct volcano.

Lion Rock reaches 650 feet or 200 metres high, and was quite a sight from the ground. The views were amazing as we climbed up; you could see the landscape for miles around. Some parts of the climb were on steel stairs on the outside of the rock, which was interesting and a little weird at the same time. You could enjoy the views, but it gave an "edge" to the climb.

It got busy and extremely hot quickly, so we arrived at 7:30 am, just after it opened. It took us about an hour to walk up as there weren't too many people when we set off, which made it a pleasant experience. There were a few different levels between steps where you could take awesome photos and a break if you needed to.

The last level has the remains of an enormous stone lion's paw, which gave us an idea of how massive this lion sculpture must have been. We wondered how on earth it was built so many years ago. The views from the top were 360 degrees, and we felt amazing once we had climbed it. You can walk up and down the layers on the top that are still intact, but most are ruins. It's quite amazing and well worth the climb.

Yoga

We did quite a bit of yoga in Sri Lanka as well. Rob was really getting into it and doing well. It's quite amazing there; yoga is a huge part of their culture so there were many yoga studios and classes to choose from. We practiced yoga nearly every day; I was in yoga heaven.

We kept up our walking and tracking our five kilometres. Rob was also running most days as well, for an hour at least.

We met an Ayurvedic doctor from one of our yoga classes and decided to have a consultation to investigate our Ayurvedic body types. After all, when in Sri Lanka, why not check out your "doshas?"

Ayurveda is short for "Ayurvedic medicine" and is one of the oldest holistic or whole-body healing systems in the world. It was developed in India more than 3000 years ago and is the traditional Hindu system of medicine. It's based on the belief that health and wellness depend on a delicate balance between the mind, body, and spirit. There are three primary doshas, which, according to Ayurveda, are the energy patterns that flow around our bodies and govern our thinking and behaviour.

The doshas are Vata, Pitta, and Kapha. We are born with all three of them, but it's the dominance of one or two that defines who we are.

We both had a consultation with Dr. Raji and that was probably the start, for me, of changing my dietary intake. I had already discovered foods that were not agreeing with me, as I experienced pain and bloating at times. I was really interested in losing weight, but wasn't achieving it. I learnt that it's not about being on a diet, it's about eating what's healthy for your body type and what benefits you. I find Ayurveda fascinating and true to self. As it turned out, I was on the right track of cutting out white wheat and most meats, but there were a few extra things my body type shouldn't eat, such as acidic foods like tomato and pineapple. Dr. Raji was great and explained why my body type couldn't tolerate certain foods. We still keep in touch today.

Rob's dietary intake never needed to change. He could eat meat, fish, veggies, drink beer – everything really, as it all agreed with his body type. Dr. Raji gave him some exercises to help strengthen his back and help with flexibility.

Typical Prices in Sri Lanka in AUD$			
Chicken Fried Rice	$6.50	String Hoppers	$0.50
Big Breakfast	$5.50	Prawn & Noodles	$8.50
Glass of White Wine	$5.50	Can of Lion Beer	$4.00
Scooter hire per day	$9.00	Casual yoga class	$10-$12
Medical: Stitches out $23.00			

MY TOP TIPS FOR PHONES

1. Ensure you have cloud-based storage for your photos. It keeps them safe and there is enough room for hundreds of photos.

2. Take a spare phone if you have one, in case it gets lost or stolen.

3. Buy a local sim card for internet if travelling far and wide. Your passport is usually required to buy a sim card.

4. Google Maps will still work out of range if you don't close it before you leave WIFI.

5. Buy a waterproof pouch that can hang around your neck if doing any water activities/tours. They are great protection for your phone and are affordable.

6. I still like to take a selfie stick or a tripod with a remote to take your own fabulous shots.

7. Turn your roaming data off whilst overseas unless you have a prepaid international plan. The rates are very high. Use WIFI instead as it's usually readily available in shops, restaurants, and cafes.

HEALTH UPDATE – WEEK 12 (April)

We were getting fitter all the time. We were exploring a lot and generally more active than we had been in years, including climbing Lion Rock, walking daily to explore, and swimming laps in the afternoons.

I was still meditating daily for about 10 minutes.

Rob was running daily and we were feeling more energised every day.

Weigh In:

Jenny – 66.1 kg   Lost 5.4 kg
Rob – 93 kg   Lost 14 kg

Exercise:

~ Walking 5-10 km daily ~   ~ yoga daily~   ~ meditation ~
~ swimming/snorkelling ~   ~ running ~

Typical Daily Food Intake:

Breakfast: Omelette, hoppers, coffee
Lunch: Prawn Salad or Chicken fried rice
Snack: Nuts and/or fresh fruit
Dinner: Prawns or chicken and vegetables
Drinks: Water and tea, occasional wine or beer

Chapter Five

Highest of the Highs

"Life is an adventure, it's not a package tour."
– Eckhart Tolle

We made our way to Kandy where we were meeting our friends, Mark and Sarah. They arrived at the airport and drove four hours to meet us, arriving at 1:30 am. We didn't get up to meet them when they arrived, so we met at breakfast. It was awesome to see familiar faces after being in some really isolated areas of Sri Lanka.

Sarah kindly brought over three much-appreciated bottles of Chandon. Yay! What a legend! Nice sparkling wine is like gold in Asia, so we sat that afternoon and enjoyed a bottle at The Flying Fox, the hotel restaurant (who graciously housed our wine in their fridge). It was wonderful to catch up and discuss our upcoming adventures.

The next morning in the hotel restaurant, a family of monkeys came in. They were investigating any food left on the tables when I turned to them and said, "Out you go, nothing here for you." The cutest one stopped and looked as though he was a child and didn't believe me, so I waved him out and said it again. It took a few more encouraging words before he believed me and left, but we could still see their tails as they scuttled off. They were just a tiny bit cute.

Our Lucky Day – Let's Drive the Train

We had a great day exploring Kandy, visiting the Temple of the Tooth (which supposedly houses a tooth of the Buddha), and watching a traditional dance show with fire walkers that night. There's quite a lot of vegan and vegetarian food in Sri Lanka, which we all enjoyed. We did so much in four days on our tour with Mark and Sarah, it felt like two weeks!

Next, we took the iconic train trip from Kandy to Ella on the blue train that goes over the Nine Arch Bridge.

This was an amazing experience; it was just our lucky day. When we were boarding the train, the train driver flagged over Tuan and me to discuss something before the train had taken off. He asked whether we would like to sit in the driver's cabin on the journey from Kandy to Ella. Huh? Hell yes. We didn't need to be asked twice. In fact, could we bring our two friends as well? Awesome.

Our driver, Tuan, left us to it and was meeting us in Ella.

The plan was we would sit in the main economy carriage that we had tickets for and wait until the driver came to signal us. I sat near the window. The seating was bench seats across with a little table in the middle, booth style. Mark and Sarah sat on the other side of the aisle over near the other window. As we got going, we were enjoying the views, and then the train came to a stop at one of the stations. The driver came to find me and said, "We will stop again in five minutes and we will signal you." I said, "Okay." I really had no idea what we were going to do or how long we were going to be in the driver's cabin for. Sure enough, we took off and after five more minutes, they stopped the train in the middle of nowhere. The man signalled to me and we picked up our bags and hurried off the train in the middle of nowhere. The other passengers looked quite perplexed to see us getting off the train; I don't think they had any idea what was going on. We grabbed Mark and Sarah, who knew nothing about this either. Luckily, they just came with us, no questions asked.

The four of us ran alongside the carriages up to the driver's cabin. We got in and with a loud toot, we were off again. We alternated sitting in the driver's seat. It was hilarious. It was like we were four big kids getting special treatment on a school excursion. I'll tell you though, you're never too old to enjoy something like this. We would have paid hundreds of dollars to actually experience a VIP-style train ride like this. So, we were sitting in the driver's seat, tooting the horn as we approached towns, tunnels, and bends in the track. We were told how many toots, how long to toot for, and when. Well, most of us got this right.

Mark made up his own rules, but promptly got scolded by the driver that his beeping was incorrect. We laughed a lot this day.

One of the funniest parts was that the train driver fell asleep! Lucky the train was on auto-pilot. The other driver was enjoying showing us the sights as we passed the valleys and towns. The views were amazing, and we could see the views clearly as we approached towns and tunnels and outside through the door windows. The drivers were both very informative when we were going through towns or over the highest mountain peak. They even told us to take photos of the sign on the peak. The lush landscape of the valleys and mountains were a sight to behold. The train ride in the highlands on the Kandy to Ella train is named as one of the most beautiful train rides in the world, and we were in the driver's cabin!

Looking out of the train on certain angles, we could see all the blue carriages, which looked amazing. As it turned out, we stayed in that carriage for the whole train ride except for the last five minutes when they stopped the train and we had to scurry back to our carriage. It was an awesome day; a day to remember.

Nine Arch Bridge

One of the highlights in the quaint village of Ella is the 30-metre-high Nine Arch Bridge. You reach it through a bit of a hike through the jungle (well, that's what Tuan called it). There were some stretches where we walked, but the rest was a scramble down dirt tracks that we slid down on foot as there was no traction. We walked and scrambled for about 30 minutes before reaching this amazing piece of architectural engineering, hidden in the lush green tea fields. As we came out of the dirt tracks, the bridge was a spectacular sight. It's a really beautiful, very old bridge, with nine arches (obviously) that carries the blue train from one side of the valley to the other. You are permitted to walk on and across the bridge (when the train isn't coming) and it really is a scene to behold.

The bridge was built in 1921 entirely out of brick, rock and cement, without a single piece of steel. It has stood solid since. According to history, the bridge was built by the locals, however the construction came to a standstill due to the lack of steel in WW1.

Trains cross the bridge about six times per day. Whilst waiting for the train, you can indulge in awesome photography which, of course, we did.

In Ella, we also saw the Ramoba Waterfalls, the Damro Tea Factory, Ravana Falls, and Adam's Peak.

Adam's Peak

When I first saw the poster in the travel tour office of GG Happy Tours, I could not believe people actually trekked up to the top of this mountain. There was no way I was going to do that. "No, thank you," I said. Rob said, "I'll have a go." So, with some more talking and discussing, I kept looking at the picture and thought, well, all sorts of people go climbing Adam's Peak to a temple at the top and locals pilgrimage to the top once a month, mostly at sunrise. So, we decided to do it.

It was huge! There are 5,500 hundred steps, mostly concrete but extremely uneven. There are high and low, long and short concrete steps; a six-and-a-half-kilometre trek from our starting point. It took three hours to get to the top and two hours to get down.

The day before the climb, we drove to Hatten, the home of Adam's Peak. It was pouring rain, and we needed to detour around a blocked road due to rally cars, which put us out by about an hour. It was a horrible road and made for a long trip. We finally got to our hotel, and were escorted up to our rooms. The rooms were built into the side of a mountain, way up from the rest of the rooms and restaurant. The steep stairs to get to our rooms just went up and up; they were relentless. The view was spectacular though; we could see Adams Peak from our room. It was a really hard climb just to get to our room, so we made sure we didn't forget anything as we didn't want to endure those stairs any more times than necessary. We all had fried rice and retired to bed early, as it was an early rise the next morning.

We left for the climb at 2 am when it was pitch black. From our hotel room, we could see Adam's Peak and the trail of street lights that lit all along the stairs to the top. Wow! "We must be nuts!" I thought as we left the room to venture to the starting point. There were small shops along the way that sold food, water, fruit, and snacks. With a Berocca, hydrolytes, water, and a banana in hand, we were off. I had a speed up/ slow down style of climbing the concrete stairs, whilst Mark and Sarah were just going at a constant pace. We drifted apart, mainly due to pace, and finally met them again at the top. We kept stopping for breaks (mostly me) and we would "leap frog" other tourists along the way, often chatting to see how they were going. It really was quite tough. Speaking to Mark and Sarah later, they said they found it an extreme physical challenge as well. "It was weird to be sweating and cold from the wind at the same time," they said. The last 100 metres were definitely the toughest. Rob pointed out the sign that read, "Nearly there – the last 100 metres" with an arrow pointing straight up. It was indeed, one hundred metres of relentless stairs that climbed straight up the peak of the mountain. There was nearly tears (mine), as we struggled up that last bit.

Once we arrived at the top, it was quite windy and extremely busy. Shoes must be removed prior to entering the top section, out of respect. There were hundreds of people strewn all over the stairs, the ground, and in the temple. What a great feeling to have achieved the climb! I was so exhausted; my face was the colour of my orange jacket.

The weather was cold and windy, so we were huddled down on the ground, covered in any spare clothing we had. When the sky began to change from the beauty of the sunrise, we all got up and moved toward the fence to see the sunrise. I was quite squished from the amount of people trying to fit on the grounds of the temple to see this magnificent sight. It truly was worth the effort to see the small, red, glowing ball of sun start to rise into view and the colours of the sky change. In the crisp, cold air, we stood and waited and watched. It was an experience that none of us will forget! And then, to climb back down.

Although I was struggling on the way up, I found my second wind on the way down and joyously skipped down. It was easy. Rob struggled a bit more on the way down. He was getting cranky as he couldn't see the finish line. We left at

2 am and we were back for breakfast at 9 am. Thousands of people go up and down Adam's Peak every single day. Some of the crowd were lovely; there were older women in a group of three, singing joyously as they walked; a group of monks walked past in matching dark red robes; and locals of all ages, some really old, just taking it one step at a time. It was absolutely amazing and worth every step.

The Van Just Stopped in the Middle of Nowhere

Speaking of interesting experiences, we broke down on the very last day in Sri Lanka after our intense climb up Adam's Peak. We'd been up since 1 am that morning, climbed Adam's Peak, had our breakfast, done some last-minute shopping, and were heading off. This is where we departed from Mark and Sarah, our adventure buddies, who had come over for four days with us. They were going to continue on in Sri Lanka, so they got our really good tour guide, Tuan, and a really reliable van. We were going a different way, heading back to Negombo to fly out the next morning, so we got a different van. As it turns out, this van was old and rattly. We were really far out in the country so there weren't any other options, and we were apparently lucky to get any van.

We were in the middle of nowhere when it started to rattle. The smoke rose from the front passenger seat, which, in a minivan, is where the engine is. That is not a good look. I said to the driver, "Smoke, smoke. What's happening?" He pulled over, the van stalled, and we got out. Rob was sleeping at the time. I thought, "Oh, this isn't good." The driver started investigating the smoke and started pouring water on the engine. Oh no, it made terrible noises and created even more smoke. Rob said, "This is not good. He doesn't know what he's doing. It's completely stuffed, there's no fixing this." The driver couldn't speak a word of English and we were pretty stuck to be honest. We sat on the rocks in the middle of nowhere for around three hours, watching the driver get very heated and argue with people on the phone, including our tour company, and the driver that Mark and Sarah had borrowed from us.

He got on the back of someone's scooter and started to head off when Rob chased him to find out what the heck was going on. Eventually, he came back with another van and a new driver. I think the first driver was sick of us. We weren't sure what was going on because nobody told us (they couldn't anyway, as they didn't speak English). We just kept sitting on the rock, waiting. (We hadn't thought about downloading a translator app onto our phones at this point.)

There were two positives though; no monkeys and no rain.

Eventually, we got a new driver with an even older van and we were just too happy to put our stuff in there and get going. Then, five minutes in, we stopped again, to meet his mother at their local shop. We are introduced to his mum because his brother is in Australia, so, knowing that we were Australians, he was very happy and proud to have us in his car. He rang numerous people and all we could understand was, "Australia, Australia." We ended up Skyping his brother as he wanted us to talk to him so he could prove that he was driving the Australians to the airport.

It wasn't his usual job. There wasn't much choice out there in a small outback town in Sri Lanka, so we were lucky to get him. All the while, we just wished to get to the hotel quickly and safely. It had been a really long day; we'd walked up Adam's Peak as well as the gazillion steps up and back from our room (which felt nearly as high as Adam's Peak). Finally, we got to Negombo at 10 pm. We had missed our day there, experiencing the lovely beachside town. The hotel manager was exceptionally nice and called the chef back to cook us a meal and get me a glass of much-needed wine.

We left at 3 am to get to the airport the next morning. The moral of that story was, never give your awesome tour driver and reliable van to your adventure buddies. We found out later, from Sarah, that the first driver blamed us for wanting the air conditioning on, which overheated the engine.

Sri Lanka is a gorgeous island and we are so glad we got to explore it, but we probably don't need to go back. The bombings in Colombo and Negombo were just after we left, so we felt blessed we left when we did.

Nearly Missed the Flight

Directly after the "break down" saga in Sri Lanka, we flew to Singapore on our way back to Bali to chill in Canggu and start booking some more adventures. We were sitting in the Singapore airport playing on our phones, totally oblivious to the time, and just about missed our flight. We ran full pace to the gate, only to realise it was the wrong way, and then ran back, with minutes to spare. I couldn't keep up. I just said to

Rob, "Run, run, and keep the gate open." He ran like mad, losing things from his backpack; it was just like the movies, but I was too stressed to laugh at that.

We must have looked a sight, though. One of the airline staff came to check I was coming and was calling me to hurry. Luckily, they kept the gate open and we got through. We finally sat down, puffing and very grateful to be on that plane. So, now what have we learnt? We set our alarm clocks in every airport to ensure that we don't miss the plane.

We stayed another week in Canggu at our boutique resort, Ecosfera, looking after our sore muscles from Adam's Peak. We were seriously sore for days.

Scooters

There are so many scooter accidents. We've been to Asia many times and we usually go only for about ten days, so you don't necessarily see many accidents. When you're there for an extended time, you start to see them and anybody can be involved, either locals or tourists. But the main culprits are the tourists. They don't wear helmets or they've never ridden a scooter before. This is evident because they go crashing out of control into the gutter, into people, or even shops.

We were watching one girl pull up on the scooter near Echo Beach. She went to park it but she kept hanging on to the accelerator on the handle, while her friend got off. Then, as she was stepping off the bike, she held the handle tightly and pulled on it, not realising it was the accelerator. So, the bike rushed forward into a local's bike, damaged it, and knocked it over. Uh oh, this wasn't good. Locals came running from everywhere. They grabbed the scooter and pried her hand off it. She was freaking out because she didn't know what was going on. Clearly, she had never ridden a scooter before.

The next minute, she and her girlfriend were at the ATM to pay this problem off. I hate to think how much that cost her. It would have cost way more than our 500,000 IDR for a red light, I'm sure.

Girls' Week

I was so excited as it was April and I hadn't really spent a lot of time chit-chatting with just my girlfriends since I saw Sarah in February. Sure, I still had a happy hour with Chrissy, on Mondays, if it worked out that way – on the phone nonetheless, but FaceTime and a wine is always good. We spoke with the family regularly, also on FaceTime, but I didn't have the girlfriend connection that I would normally have had at work, at home, at yoga, or wherever. It didn't stress me out, but I was absolutely looking forward to seeing the girls – Suez, Chrissy, and Jan – and just enjoying "girl time."

The first night they arrived, we had so much to say that we lost track of time and stayed in our rooms. We booked rooms that had a lap pool where the terrace or balcony would be. They were fantastic. We put music on, danced, drank, and had a ball. We ended up staying in with room service. It poured down rain, so we even stood in the rain and sang; not sure what the neighbours thought, but we had a great night.

We spent a week enjoying the sun, the beach, shopping, and day trips. We went on an e-bike tour through the rice fields of Ubud, had lunch afterwards, and went on the big swing. The best thing about this tour was that the bike also had a small electric motor that would pull you up the hills if needed. I wasn't that fit yet, so I used the motor. It was awesome riding through the vibrant green rice fields enjoying the fresh air. The paths were a little too narrow at some points, but no one fell in the fields. I would probably never go again without a motorised bike; the hills are quite steep.

Many a night we had drinks on the beach at sunset, chatting, and enjoying the beach atmosphere. We had so much fun just catching up and enjoying time out.

Rob flew to Patong Beach again to do some more Muay Thai boxing. Any time out he had, he headed over to his favourite place. He loved the rustic lifestyle of Patong, the relaxed atmosphere, and the locals. The locals, too, were beginning to know him and welcome him back. He went to a small local bar that had a pool competition and a BBQ night they invited him to. I remember he texted me to say he had won the pool competition. "Excellent, I hope you got prize money," I said, thinking yes, how exciting, he's a pool shark. This is great! But no – he'd won just enough to play again.

Meet You Back in Canggu for Our Next Visitors

Rob flew back to Bali in time to see the girls off and we headed back to Canggu to wait for our friends Rhonda and Ian to arrive. Chrissy stayed another night to experience Canggu and stay with us a little longer. Rhonda and Ian got to the Denpasar airport, where our driver collected them. I had organised three different locations to stay with them; Canggu, Ubud, and Nusa Lembongan – all of our favourites. I even created them an itinerary from "Jen's Tours" and emailed to them before they left. (See Appendix A.)

Ian is also an experienced motorbike rider, so the boys hired scooters and went exploring. Rhonda and I caught up over a few cocktails by the pool. It was great to catch up and show them around. They said they would never have come to Bali if we weren't there, as it wasn't somewhere they wanted to navigate on their own.

We went to our favourite restaurants in Canggu including Tropikale, Deus, Old Mans, and Ecosfera Green Spot Café. We did a little shopping, exploring on the scooters, walking every morning, and a little yoga.

Typical Prices in Bali in AUD$			
Nasi Goreng	$5.50	Chicken & Veggies	$8.50
Big Breakfast	$5.50	Prawn & Noodles	$8.50
Glass of White Wine	$8.50	Bintang Beer	$2.50
Scooter hire per day	$6.00	Casual yoga class	$12.00

MY TOP MONEY TIPS

1. Never take all your cash out with you.

2. Don't let vendors see your cash in your wallet; the price will instantly increase.

3. Leave a credit or cash card at the hotel as a back-up.

4. Get a fee-free travel card from your bank before you leave to avoid ATM fees.

5. Advise your bank that you are travelling overseas so they don't lock your card.

6. Check the exchange rates before you go. It's often a better rate in the country than at the airports.

7. Download a currency converter app to convert your prices to your own currency or take a small note with the conversions written on them for ease when bargaining. It can get confusing when bartering.

HEALTH UPDATE – WEEK 16 (April)

We had climbed Adam's Peak and were feeling fit and energetic.

I had my girls' week in Bali, and relaxed some of the good habits I'd made by indulging in cocktails and pasta (although we were still fairly active and walked a lot).

Rob was running daily, boxing, and working out at a gym. He was really enjoying keeping fit and improving his fitness. Now, he wanted to include more muscle strengthening routines.

Weigh In:

Jenny – 65.5 kg   Lost 6 kg
Rob – 90 kg   Lost 17 kg

Exercise:

~ Walking 5-10 km daily ~   ~ yoga ~   ~ meditation ~
~ swimming ~   ~ running ~

Typical Daily Food Intake:

Breakfast: Eggs or smoothies, fruit, coffee
Lunch: Chicken and cashew nuts, prawn salad
Snack: Nuts and/or fresh fruit
Dinner: Prawns, chicken and vegetables, or pasta
Drinks: Water and tea (and many cocktails)

Chapter Six

Cranking up the Fitness

"Don't be afraid to try something new."
– Dell Curry

Next stop – Ubud

In Ubud, we rode to the Tegenungan Waterfall, which Rhonda and Ian loved. Rhonda went on the big swing and we climbed to the top of the hill to explore the stream that fed the waterfall. It's beautiful up there just watching the water cascade down the cliff side, spraying mist everywhere. It's very serene.

We explored on the way home, stopping at various factories and warehouses with homewares and glass planters, large statues, and more. It was extremely hot, and we had to stop and put sunscreen on a few times and buy extra water. Rhonda and I had fun shopping at the Ubud markets while the boys went off somewhere. Ian was a little ill, so Rhonda, Rob, and I went out to the markets for some last-minute purchases, and all three of us rode home on the scooter. Not saying that's a good thing but it was funny. We stayed at Merthayasa Bungalow II homestay, swam in the pool, and enjoyed the family-like environment.

Rhonda and Ian had come over to engage in our festivities and wanted to go to the Monkey Forest in Ubud. "Be my guest, but don't think for a minute, I will come with you," I told them. Rhonda couldn't believe I was scared of monkeys. They are not cute.

*****

The last stop was Nusa Lembongan. We stayed at Dream Beach Huts on Dream Beach. It is a beautiful place with an infinity pool, bar, and restaurant. We had stayed there in February and knew Rhonda and Ian would love it. You don't really need to leave the resort, but we did go exploring on the scooter to the far end of the island.

We decided to go snorkelling with the manta rays. We had heard about it last time we were here but didn't do it. So, when Rhonda and Ian came over, we thought they'd love it as they're quite adventurous too. It was an amazing experience. These creatures are so graceful, quiet, and inquisitive. They're massive; their wingspan reaches six or seven feet wide, but they are very graceful, so don't panic. As we approached the area with many other boats, you could see them from the boat. We got in the rough water and soon enough they were swimming up to us, just as curious about us as we were about them.

They had no problem with coming right up underneath you, as they must be comfortable with all the tourists swimming there. We were a bit nervous of touching them with our flippers though, so we were trying to curl our legs up and keep away from them, but then they came even closer. They were beautiful, magnificent creatures. They don't sting; they don't have a stinger tail like a stingray, even though they look similar. It was an amazing experience.

It was also Rob's birthday, so it was a great birthday gift. Ian was feeling a little green under the gills, but was such a good sport to continue on with this adventure even though the rough boat ride didn't agree with him. I think he slept for hours when we got back. Rhonda is very creative, so she spent ages coming up with ideas for Rob's birthday present. In the end, she decided on a fresh frangipani lei as a gift. However, there weren't enough flowers around, so she decided to climb the closest frangipani tree to shake the flowers free for his birthday. I laughed so hard at this sight and the many flowers that were now on the ground.

When Rob woke in the morning, there was a "Happy Birthday Rob" sign written in frangipani petals on the grass in front of our hut. There were also balloons tied to the door and balcony. He was amazed and so grateful at her thoughtful gesture.

Soon enough, "Jen's Tours" came to an end, and we flew home with Rhonda and Ian to stop in for a few days to celebrate birthdays and Mother's Day.

*****

It was weird stopping at home. It didn't really feel like home because we hadn't finished our trip yet. I took this opportunity to swap clothes though. I got sick of wearing the same things constantly, so the change of clothes was nice. We needed to buy Rob new clothes as he was still losing weight. This was our last stop at home until the end of the trip.

When we were home in March, I was looking at flights and decided we would fly to Byron Bay to check it out. We had never been there, and most people from Philip Island go there regularly, so I thought it was a good opportunity, especially as the flights were cheap.

Byron Bay

It was May and not that warm, but probably warmer than Melbourne. We stayed in a cabin in a park within walking distance to the main street and the beach. The beach is beautiful there. There was an old local guy raking patterns into the sand, and it was quite amazing and very creative, I could've watched him for hours. I assume he is there a lot, raking his creations in the sand. The town has a great vibe and the yoga is good there too. We had a favourite bar near where we stayed, which was recommended to us, called the Railway Friendly Bar. It had great food and live bands most nights.

While we were in Byron Bay, we were thinking of what to do next in our trip. I found some yoga and boxing camps online and sent the link to Rob. After some Googling, he found a Muay Thai Boxing camp a four-hour drive north of Bangkok. It sounded good, so I searched for flights to Bangkok. We got some cheap flights for the day after we got back from Byron Bay. The last day there was the sunniest day we'd seen.

Rob was keeping fit; everywhere we went, he found a gym and got a week's pass. I tried a couple of yoga classes, but mostly I got so in-depth in a book I was reading that I didn't do much exercise. Rob trained for this boxing camp and later said, "I can't believe you did nothing to prepare while I was running my ass off, and you managed fine at the boxing camp." Actually, I was surprised myself.

The next day we flew back to Melbourne Airport, stayed the night at the Park Royal Hotel, and flew out for Bangkok in the morning.

Boxing Camp #1 – Battle Conquer Gym

Rob booked this camp and chose a seven-day wellness and boxing package. It was full on. It was in dusty, dry, hot country four hours' drive north of Bangkok in Petchuban. Battle Conquer Gym was originally a family farm that housed a gym for local boxers to use for training. It was a great local community, where you got to know the extended family living nearby. The gym had grown and extended into a camp for locals and tourists. It was owned and run by the landowner's daughter, Noi, and managed by a westerner, Lucy, who decided to stay on after originally training there.

As we approached the gym, the first thing we thought was, "Where the hell are we?" There was nothing in sight except the occasional old farm house and rice fields, which weren't as beautiful and green at that time of the year. It was so hot, easily 43 degrees. The bed was as hard as a rock and the showers were only cold water. It was rustic. We like rustic holidays, but my lordy, this was *rustic*.

We did two classes of Muay Thai per day; two hours in the morning, 7 am till 9 am, and the later session was 3 pm till 5 pm. The training sessions were relentless. It started with an hour of warm up (well, I was worn out already), then the boxing drills, and then stretching to cool down. We began to dislike the warm ups as they were constant cycles of running, burpees, sit ups, skipping, side stepping – truly exhausting. I think they were trying to wear us out before we even boxed. We did drills against the boxing bags, drills with the trainers, and drills in pairs. We had both boxed a little before, but wanted to start in the ring as beginners, learning basic techniques. We bought hand wraps to protect our knuckles and hands, and learnt how to wrap them around our hands, but I got the trainers to do it for me. It wasn't long before they had us boxing in pairs with other guests, not each other. The private lessons with the trainers were really beneficial to developing our skills. The staff were all very helpful and patient. New guests arrived daily, so the skill sets were varied within the group.

I've come to an age where I don't want to sleep on a hard bed that felt like wood, especially after a day of exhausting exercise. My muscles were so sore and then my hips got really sore on this plank of wood they called a bed. We only had a sheet and two pillows, so we scrounged up any sort of quilt to pad out an area to lie on. I made a slim, sleeping bag sized area that I could lie on that would help my poor old body cope with the hardness of the bed. But it is Thailand; that is how they have their beds. They don't always have a mattress anyway. Of course, Rob was fine.

On about day four, the manager on site, Lucy, sent us texts to keep in touch. She said, "How are you going?" And I said, "We're going well, it's a challenge but I'm not sleeping well because the bed is so hard. Do you have any other beds we can try?" To my utter surprise, she said, "Okay, I'll try and get you a new bed," and promptly ordered me a new mattress. Rob and I just looked at each other; we couldn't believe it. "Wow, this is good service," we said. Not many other people there got service like that.

We got our new bed and guess what? It was as hard as the other bed. It's just the way they make their local beds in Thailand. So, I padded this one up and didn't complain because she did her best to accommodate my needs.

The food was local produce and it was freshly cooked by their own chefs. As long as you liked rice, chicken, and vegetables, you were fine, because that was the staple diet for brunch and dinner. There was some variance in the way it was presented, but it was rice, chicken, and vegetables, nonetheless.

However, we were really hungry from exercising so much that we ate two serves. I never thought I would be eating lukewarm vegetables including cauliflower for breakfast, but I did and enjoyed every mouthful.

There were many activities on offer at this camp, not just two-hour classes morning and night. There were other options. You could do bootcamp, cross-fit, or a "Buddha run" in the morning instead of boxing training if you chose. One morning I decided on the Buddha run while Rob stayed at the boxing session. They took a group of us in a ute up to the big Buddha to run up and down the steps as many times as you could, counting laps and timing yourself. The rest of the group would cheer you on. It was good, but exhausting. I think I made it up and down 17 times; quite an effort, considering the most was 21. I was happy with that.

We researched another boxing camp that was recommended to us; Bangarang Gym in Chiang Mai. My lordy, it looked like a five-star resort. There was no comparison. It looked beautiful. We kept that in mind in case we wanted to try another camp, but said, "Let's just finish this one first."

Brunch was served in the café at 9:30 am and dinner at 6 pm. The middle of the day was the hottest and there were several options; rest up, massage, swim at the local pool, or a cultural activity like meditating at the nearby temple. We chose to hire a scooter and go for coffee at a western-style coffee shop in any spare time we got. That was our treat. Hot chips and coffee – it doesn't sound much but when you're in outback Thailand, it feels like home.

Yoga was included every second day which really helped our sore muscles too. Thinking about the amount of activity, it really was a challenge, especially coming from not much of an exercise routine.

It was about 43 degrees outside the tin shelter that housed the Muay Thai boxing and even hotter inside. On two occasions a tropical storm came through, which was a nice relief from the heat. We stood out in the rain to cool down, and it was very welcome.

We had three massages included in our package and we used every one of those, plus a few extras. Boy oh boy, do your muscles get sore. We were exhausted. Even the hard bed was no problem after a few days because I was that exhausted, I just fell asleep anyway. The showers were cold, which was quite refreshing. At night, after dinner, we would just have a walk around the rice fields and retire pretty early because we'd be up again at 6:30 am getting ready for boxing in the morning.

What we learnt to appreciate was to use electrolytes in our drinks. This rehydrates you so that you can keep going, otherwise, you just get too exhausted. Electrolytes and Berocca became our best friends right through this boxing camp.

It was awesome fun and we were so inspired and rejuvenated that I really did think I wanted to do another one. I didn't manage to do the two boxing sessions every day, but Rob did most, if not all of them. The trainers were all amazing, really fun, and great teachers.

There weren't many couples at this camp, mostly singles and people younger than us. That never deters us though, because we had each other and know that age is just a number.

The boxing camp was one of the main highlights of the trip; we were so glad we chose it and it raised our fitness regime to the next level.

Hua Hin

We thought we would book a week at Hua Hin as my friends, Chrissy and Kim, had stayed there the previous year and really enjoyed it. I checked with them before booking and was reassured we would like it.

We booked a driver to take us to Hua Hin, which was a seven-hour car ride from Petchuban. We stopped a few times for petrol and food. The driver was very nice, but didn't speak much English. It cost AUD $236 for the transfer. It's probably really cheap if we consider a seven-hour car transfer in Melbourne. It would cost us more to get to the airport from home (Philip Island) which takes approximately 2.5 hours.

We originally headed down south of Bangkok to Hua Hin, thinking we would need a week to recover, but soon realised we liked the training schedule and how fit we were becoming.

The most fun in Hua Hin were the night markets where we ate great street food, which was awesome and cheap. It's while we were there that we reflected on how much fun we had and how fit and healthy we felt. We thought we would book another boxing camp. Rob said, "Are you keen to do another camp?" I said, "Absolutely." So, we booked the next boxing camp for August in a couple of months' time.

We stayed at another IBIS hotel in Hua Hin; this one was dog-friendly. We couldn't believe the dogs and their belongings that were checking in. It looked like something from Beverley Hills in a movie. The dogs were carried by their owners, dressed in their tiaras, whilst their vast array of accessories were wheeled in on a suitcase trolley. There were fluffy pink beds, dog cages, cat kennels, leads with diamantes. It was quite a sight. The entire third floor was to accommodate guests and their pets. I have never seen or heard of a hotel accepting pets before. We didn't hear any barking so the walls must have been sound-proof.

We hired scooters at most of the places we stayed to get around and explore easier. Sometimes, I took a while to acclimatise to the traffic and mayhem on a scooter but usually I was ok. We hired a scooter from the hotel for the week. Rob was pulled over in a traffic check, on the highway. Luckily, he always takes his licence with him now, so that was checked, no problem.

There was one other problem though; the scooter was out of registration by two months. Rob had to pay a 400 Thai Baht fine to leave the police and get back to the hotel. It was lucky he had that much money on him, due to our budget restrictions. Back at the hotel, the registration papers were still sitting in the top drawer, not paid. Oops. The hotel fixed the problem, paid Rob back, and off he went again.

The best part of Hua Hin was the delicious, fresh street food at the night markets. We went most nights to indulge in different foods. Delicious! They also had colourful locally-made, hand-crafted creations.

A three-hour car ride back to the Bangkok Airport and we were off again – this time to Phuket, just a one-hour domestic flight.

Typical Prices in Phuket in AUD$			
Chicken Cashew Nuts	$6.00	Chicken & Veggies	$8.50
Big Breakfast	$5.50	Prawn & Noodles	$8.50
Glass of White Wine	$9.00	Bintang Beer	$2.50
Scooter hire per day	$7.50	Casual yoga class	$12.00
Massage $12.00 – 15.00			

TOP GENERAL TIPS WHILST TRAVELLING IN ASIA

1. Always take hand sanitizer and tissues with you at all times.

2. Have your "can do" attitude with you when trying new things.

3. Only drink bottled water in Asian countries.

4. When booking online, look for "no deposit/ payment" bookings, in case you change your direction.

5. Check what the climate is like before you get there, and be prepared with clothing etc.

6. Always take snacks if travelling a lot or on tours. Protein bars, nuts, or fruit will keep the hunger attacks at bay.

7. Take probiotics or Yakult daily to protect your gut health.

HEALTH UPDATE – WEEK 21 (May)

We felt fit and healthier. We just completed our first boxing camp which was amazing and fitness focused. There was no drinking or junk food.

We were both hooked on keeping fit now we had completed this challenge and enjoyed the energy we now had. It was easy to eat well and not venture "off the wagon."

It was so hot we introduced Berocca and hydrolytes to help rehydrate.

Weigh In:

Jenny – 64.5 kg   Lost 7 kg | Rob – 88 kg   Lost 19 kg

Exercise:

~ Walking 5-10 km daily ~   ~ yoga ~   ~ meditation ~
~ running ~   ~ boxing ~

Typical Daily Food Intake:

Breakfast: Eggs, toast, coffee
Lunch: Chicken, rice, vegetables
Snack: Nuts and/or fresh fruit
Dinner: Prawns or chicken and vegetables
Drinks: Water, hydrolytes, and Berocca

Leaving. Yay!

Jenny and Sarah at the Taj Mahal, India

Sarah and Jenny at Rishikesh Yoga Retreat

Elephant spotting near Arugam Bay

Train ride to Ella in Sri Lanka in the driver's cabin

Nine Arch Bridge, Sri Lanka with Mark and Sarah

Adam's Peak with Mark and Sarah

Ebike tour, girls' week, Ubud

Jen on big swing in Ubud

Three on the bike – Rob, Jen, Rhonda

With Rhonda and Ian at the Tegenungan Waterfall Ubud

Happy to have survived our first boxing
camp at Battle Conquer

Ziplining, Phuket with the Dares

James Bond Island tour with Phoebe

At Deus Café, Canggu with Sue and Dave

The winning longboard

Dave and Rob exploring Ubud rice terraces

Special treatment for Jen at Bangarang boxing training

Rob with his new boxing moves at Bangarang

Rob fighting fit – at Bangarang Gym

Elephant Sanctuary in Chiang Mai, Thailand

With Ryan and Airi in Fukuoka, Japan

Japan, Typhoon Krosa with Ryan and Airi

Fave photo, fave place – Phuket

Just one drink at Mookies Bar

Graduated as yoga teachers with Christie

Always carry your international licence or a lot of cash

Before and after – Jen

Before and after – Rob

Chapter Seven

The Pad in Patong

"Freedom is priceless."
– Damon Dash

During recent visits to Patong Beach, Rob had looked around for cheaper accommodation that could be suitable for our stay. He had seen one hotel called Boomerang Inn which was in a good location, so he booked it for the first two nights. We would look around for somewhere else if it wasn't suitable for our planned stay of one month.

We decided that it wasn't quite suitable for such an extended stay, so we walked around the area and took photos of the hotels I liked the look of. We went back and looked online for the prices. Gone are the days of just booking in at reception; it doesn't happen anymore, it's all online. We have even booked hotels online while sitting in their foyer, as the staff won't take reservations. We had looked at the Aspery Hotel and thought it would be suitable for a whole month and very affordable at AUD $27 per night including breakfast. It was much cheaper than I first thought. This was exciting, as we knew we wanted to stay for an extended period in just one place and Patong was a favourite.

For the entire month of June, we stayed at Aspery Hotel and it felt like home. The staff were happy to see us each morning. The waiter made me my favourite breakfast each morning ready for when we arrived. We knew the massage girls downstairs, Mia at the tour desk, Ida in the coffee shop nearby, and the family at our local favourite restaurant.

*****

We flew to Singapore in mid-June for two reasons; I wanted Rob to see the stunning architecture there and it was the easiest way to avoid overstaying our tourist visa in Phuket. Many people extend their tourist visa, and we could have done that, but as we wanted to visit Singapore anyway, we thought we'd go for a few days. We didn't need to take much, so we left our case and other belongings at the hotel until we returned. I had collected extra things by now, including a yoga mat and towels, large drink bottles for the gym, and protein shake powder (in a huge container), which we didn't need to take to Singapore.

We stayed at Novotel in Clarke Quay, where I have been before. It's on the Singapore river, so we would walk along the river amongst the buzz of cafes, restaurants, and live bands. The nightlife is very cool along there.

We took the water taxi up along the river to Marina Bay, taking photos as we approached the Marina Bay Sands Hotel area. The Marina Bay Sands is Singapore's most iconic hotel containing the world's largest rooftop infinity pool. The architecture is amazing. We had a drink at the rooftop bar where the view is incredible, especially at sunset. You can walk around most of it but not in the pool area, as it's for guests only. AUD $22 will buy you a ticket to enter the rooftop bar and that becomes credit you can spend on drinks when you get up there. Rob ordered bubbles and a beer – a total of AUD $45, just above our ticket credit. The view was amazing though and we went in the afternoon to catch the sunset. The views of the river and the Gardens by the Bay trees were awesome.

Then we wandered over to the Gardens by the Bay to see the metal trees lit up at night. The light show is on every night with free entry. There are suspended walking tracks between the trees which are quite high and the view is amazing. The "Supertrees" are tree-like structures 25 to 50 metres tall. They are solar-powered and truly magnificent. The lights dance to the music of the "Garden Rhapsody" theme and the dazzling show lasts for fifteen minutes. The gardens and the hotel were busy with tourists but it's definitely worth a visit.

*****

Back in Phuket, we started out by getting a personal trainer each at the gym for ten sessions. We then joined the gym, Maximum Fitness, for a month and started our routine of living in Patong.

Rob organised a personal trainer, Miss Chom, twice a week for the month. Miss Chom is a bodybuilder and a personal trainer and had Rob working hard from the beginning. He quickly had a daily routine to work on different muscle groups and really enjoyed the gym workouts. I had Miss Deer as my personal trainer for a few sessions. We went to the gym almost daily.

We hired a scooter from the hotel to be sure it was checked regularly, and we could get petrol and our washing done there as well. Washing was done overnight and cost was approximately AUD $2.50 per kilo, and a little more if you wanted it ironed as well. We were happy with that.

We had a great routine:

- Breakfast
- Walk
- Swim in the pool
- Gym
- Lunch
- Chill out – avoiding the afternoon sun by reading, watching videos, or maybe a trip to the shops
- Another swim
- Walk to the beach for dinner
- Maybe a game of pool at the local reggae bar after dinner

This was a fabulous daily routine and we loved staying near the beach, eating well, keeping fit, and enjoying the warmer climate. It was a great constant routine of exercise, relaxation, and enjoyment while also becoming fitter and stronger than ever.

We met some really interesting people at the Maximum Fitness gym while we were there. We went nearly every day at varying times and met lots of different people. Some lived in Patong and some came frequently as FIFOs (fly-in fly-out workers from the oil rigs). One guy, Mick, came over every two weeks he was off work and enjoyed the laidback lifestyle of Phuket. He'd even had surgery in Patong to remove excess skin after losing 55 kg; we know this for a fact, as he showed us his scars. Some people like to share way too much!

During our time at Patong, we got to know the locals at the restaurants on the beach and also some of the vendors that sold their products on a daily basis. They relentlessly walked up and down the beach day and night (fully clothed from head to toe even on scorching hot days) to earn enough money to send home to their families. They are sent over to Phuket by their parents from the very young age of 15. Their stories are amazing and it's hard to believe people live like this, but they do what they can for their families.

Their products included: sunglasses, flower leis, jewellery, art, clothing, and a whole lot of other cheaply made items. There are a lot of younger kids selling products, probably as they are cheaper labour, but it's amazing to watch the territorial traits of the older vendors towards the younger ones. It's heartbreaking to see them lose the light in their eyes when we know children of the same age who would never have to endure this kind of life.

The older boys that sold the sunglasses came from other countries, usually Cambodia or Laos, and had a great time relating to us as we saw them so much. They became like long-lost friends, a familiar face, a friendly smile perhaps, and would even run up to us randomly when we were walking along the beach.

It's the mayhem and madness we love about Patong Beach, particularly at night time. The six or seven jet skis in a row, towed behind a four-wheel drive ute, sometimes littered with youngsters, sometimes not. At sunset, it's crazy with tourists going parasailing, people blowing whistles and shouting for you to get out of the way, or staying still while they land on the beach. We love it all; the crazy vibes, the crazy people, and the coloured sky.

My new favourite cocktail became the Lychee Martini – oh my god, they're good! I think they've just got three ingredients: vodka, lychees, and lychee juice from the can. Time and again, I would sit at sunset drinking one of these, thanking my lucky stars.

We met tourists along the way, including a brother and sister from Germany. They were dining at the same restaurant as us when the waiter told us they wanted us to join them for a drink. Well, why not? They were only in their twenties but happy to chat, have a few drinks, and have a laugh.

Whilst in Thailand, I felt the need to have my eyebrows microbladed (not that I even knew that's what it was called at the time) as my eyebrows are so fair you can hardly see them in photos. We saw a salon that did eyebrows and I went in to enquire about the cost and procedure. Rob was surprised because I hadn't mentioned it before, but his reaction was, "Well Jen, when in Thailand… the land of beauty nips and tuck. Why not get it done here?" So, I did.

The process involves cutting hairlike strokes with a microblade on your eyebrows and then adding pigment to the cuts to create the illusion of more hairs. This adds colour and shape, and looks quite natural. They put numbing cream on my eyebrows, which was awesome – there was no pain at all, just some tugging at my eyebrow area. I'm pretty happy with the result and my spontaneous decision.

*****

The coffee shop under the hotel was one of our favourite hangouts. You could often find us just lounging on their couch reading or watching our phones, enjoying a western-style cappuccino. The staff here were women of three generations –grandmother, mother, and daughter – and they were all really nice and welcoming. They got to know our order and began making our coffees as soon as we entered the lovely, air-conditioned café. Rob often ordered a ham and salad roll, similar to a Subway roll, which was really expensive for Thailand, but sometimes you just need to be reminded of home; AUD $13, but really delicious.

Missing Family and Friends

I remember it was a Monday and we had just been FaceTiming Matthew and Brittany, and things were going really well for them. They were pregnant and had just signed the contract to build their first home. They were showing us their plans and pictures of how their house would look, which was super exciting. It was a great call, discussing all of their plans and we were so proud and happy they were sharing this with us. But

I felt miserable all day, thinking that we were missing some huge milestones in their lives. We hadn't seen them since May (which was probably not that long ago, really) but it was the first time I remember feeling homesick and missing the family.

We FaceTimed all of our kids at different stages and times throughout the trip. Ryan and Airi were in Japan, so it was great to keep up with where they were and how they were settling into life there. Hailey and Clayton (the younger two) were back in Melbourne and keeping us up to date on their lives too. We had previously taken all of our kids to Phuket in Thailand on holidays, so it was good that they could relate to where we were and what we were doing in Thailand.

It was awesome that we could keep in touch so easily. But we had never left home for months at a time, ever. So, dealing with the absence of seeing family was difficult sometimes. Mostly, we knew everyone was fine, so we were too.

We also caught up with friends on a regular basis as we were missing them too. It was wonderful when friends came over to spend time with us. And soon, Mark and Sarah would be back in town.

TOP TIPS TO KEEP YOU CONNECTED

1. Make sure your loved ones have the same communication apps ready to use on their phones.

2. Use a video app – it's great to "see" how everyone is going.

3. WhatsApp is a popular app used to communicate with local drivers or accommodation in most Asian countries.

4. Download a translation app on your phone if you'll be in areas where you don't speak the language.

5. Take a business card from the hotel to give to the taxi driver if you can't speak their language.

6. Leave a copy of your itinerary with your family.

HEALTH UPDATE – WEEK 24 (June)

We had just spent the whole month in Patong engaging in a routine of gym workouts in addition to our now normal daily exercise routines.

We both had personal trainers from Maximum Fitness gym and worked out daily, concentrating on more weight lifting and strength training.

I stabilised in weight here while Rob pushed himself with the gym workouts to increase his overall strength.

Weigh In:

Jenny – 64.5 kg   Lost 7 kg
Rob – 86 kg Lost 21 kg

Exercise:

~ Walking 5-10 km daily ~   ~ yoga ~   ~ meditation ~
~ running ~   ~ gym weights and strength routines ~

Typical Daily Food Intake:

Breakfast: Eggs, toast, coffee
Lunch: Basil chicken, chicken fried rice
Snack: Nuts and/or fresh fruit
Dinner: Prawns or chicken and vegetables
Drinks: Water, tea, hydrolytes, and protein shakes

Chapter Eight

No Lonely Planet

"Laughter is an instant vacation."
– Milton Berle

Phuket with the Dares

July school holidays gave the Dares good reason to come and experience "Jen's Tours." They wanted to meet us in Phuket to see why we loved it so much. Mark, Sarah, and their children, Naish, Phoebe, and her boyfriend Elliott, all came to spend time with us. It was a hoot!

During their visit, we spent four nights in Patong Beach and four nights at Kata Beach. We went to the Big Buddha, ziplining, James Bond Island, shopping in the "back" rooms, sunset drinks at Ska Bar, and surfing at Kata Beach. I think Mark still carries an injury from surfing at Kata Beach, or so he mentions every time we see him.

On their first night, the boys all went to "fight night," which Patong Beach is renowned for. Fight night is quite a commercialised boxing night in a stadium with competition fighters; it's held every other night at the Bangla stadium. Mark, Rob, and Naish (Elliott hadn't arrived yet) left dinner to go to fight night, leaving Sarah, Phoebe, and I to drink more wine at the restaurant, thinking we would meet them back at the hotel. We hadn't caught up since February and had a lot of stories to tell. I had missed the girly chats, so we stayed drinking half-decent wine and cocktails until the restaurant closed. We were walking home when Rob found us; he was worried when he didn't find us at home. Oops – we were having such a good time we didn't realise it was already midnight.

If you've ever been shopping in Phuket, you'll know about the "back" rooms. These rooms are where the shop owners keep their "good" fake copies of items such as Gucci handbags and wallets, Tiffany jewellery, sunglasses, and clothing that they don't want on display at the street front.

Policing of these illegal items is random, so they keep the prized possessions out of sight waiting for interested shoppers to come along. We thought the Dares would find it interesting to see. Years ago, they had many back rooms for pirated CDs. We used to be taken into hidden, air-conditioned rooms with CDs that lined the walls – there were thousands of them. We always found it amazing and a little amusing, as we never saw this at home.

*****

Freedom Beach is an oasis, a hidden gem near Patong Beach. It's not publicised, but Rob was exploring one day on the scooter and came across a very small sign and followed the track. We had been there previously and thought our adventure buddies would love to see it too. We hired a minivan to drive us to the car park. No cars or scooters could get any further due to the damaged track with huge cracks in it. We walked up to a cyclone fence with a locked gate.

To access the pathway, you needed to climb under the fence. I'm not sure if that was legal, but it made for an interesting adventure. The beach has that aqua water you see on Instagram photos (I nearly said postcard – but that's showing my age!) with beautiful sand and awesome palm trees. It was unspoilt and idyllic. It is quite a walk along the track with overgrown grass on either side and it's a bit jungle-like, but as you start to get closer, there are glimpses through the trees of the amazing water.

It is a real oasis. The tide was in, so we had to climb over the rocks to access the beach, but it was well worth it. There are no vendors at this beach (they're prohibited) which makes it more special as it remains unspoilt. We swam and stayed on the beach till it got too hot and unbearable and then headed back to the hotel pool. It's well worth a visit.

Ziplining

We love the chance to take people ziplining in Phuket. They have 28 platforms that you zipline between in the rainforest, just out of Patong. The views are sensational, the guides are entertaining and helpful, and the safety procedures improve each time we go.

You walk up a spiral staircase, across bridges, and then abseil down the last pole. It takes about two hours to complete and is well worth the AUD $100 (if you like heights). So we booked for all of us to go, even though Sarah was a little concerned about the height of the platforms. We went through a brief safety check, put on our harnesses and helmets, took the obligatory photos, and then headed out onto the platforms. There was a fair amount of walking and climbing to get to some platforms.

Our group was just the seven of us, which was fun. Sarah's first zipline was her scariest I'm sure; her face was filled with terror and when she made her first landing, she hugged the tree in the centre of the platform until her fingers were white. It took her a while to relax her grip enough to let go. She was fine after that. Naish went "Superman" style by clipping the cable to his back; he was lying down facing the forest floor while in a Superman pose and flew off on the zipline with one of the guides. It looked like fun, but not for me!

James Bond Island Tour

Another fun day was going out to James Bond Island. We booked the long slow boat which has a buffet lunch on board. It's a great day out; we stopped four or five times at different locations to investigate, swim, or canoe through the caves.

The small needle-shaped island is officially called Tapu, but it's known as James Bond Island because it appeared in the

1974 movie "The Man with the Golden Gun." It's an over-commercialised island, as there are only a few local markets and the tiniest beach there with thousands of daily visitors, but it's really just to grab tourists' attention.

We stopped twice to go kayaking through the caves in Phang Nga Bay. There are many local guides waiting in kayaks to greet you at the boat and take two or three tourists with them in and out of the caves. This has to be done at low tide, as the cave entrance is totally blocked at high tide. We had a freshly cooked buffet lunch then stopped for a swim in the bay. Phoebe came in our kayak, as they were taking three people per kayak. She got mistaken for our daughter, which we happily went along with.

The landscape, or should I say, seascape is absolutely incredible – we can never get enough of it. Phang Nga Bay's breathtaking scenery stretches out over an area of almost 500 square kilometres. Thirty miles northeast from Phuket, it is famous for its "hongs," which translates as "rooms." These tall, sandstone islands have collapsed in the middle, and the cliffs that formed inside surround lagoons, which, depending on the tides, can be explored by kayaks.

We entered these lagoons via cave entrances, paddled by very experienced kayak guides who pointed out interesting rock formations. Once we were inside the lagoons, which housed many mangrove trees, the atmosphere became calm and serene. When you look up through the huge sandstone walls that open to the sky, it feels very surreal, as though you're standing in the crater of a long-extinct volcano.

It was an amazing experience and one we keep taking friends back to as it's not quite like any other experience. Countless sandstone formations rise up vertically out of the sea, up to 350 metres high – a sight that can't be found anywhere else in the world.

*****

We love going to the Ska Bar at Kata beach, especially at sunset. It's a very rustic reggae bar nestled at the trunk of a huge old tree at the end of Kata Beach. We also frequented an awesome restaurant called Unnis at Kata Beach near where we were staying that served awesome vegan and vegetarian food and 99 baht (AUD $4.50) cocktails. I think we went through the cocktail list numerous times!

Mark, Sarah, and gang left for the airport from Novotel Kata Beach and we had one last night back at Patong Beach, before we headed off again.

Off to Bali to Meet Sue and Dave

The day after Mark and Sarah left, we flew back to Bali to meet Sue and Dave (Rob's sister and partner) in Canggu. They messaged us a few months back to say they were going in July. We love catching up with them so we booked flights and met them there. One of our favourite places is La Brisa, in Canggu; a rustic beach club with a "shipwreck" theme. It's stunning, especially at sunset. We met there for drinks on our first night.

For this trip, we chose a lovely homestay called Mikuk just up from Batu Bolong Beach, owned by the lovely Nuri. On the first morning, we were just awake and still in bed when their dog started barking madly. We didn't take any notice at first, until the glass doors started rattling loudly and the floor began shaking for what felt like a minute, but was only recorded as 15 seconds. We looked at each other puzzled, and Rob said, "Wow, I think it's an earthquake."

We Googled it, and sure enough, an earthquake of 5.8 magnitude struck Bali at 8:16 am – it wasn't just our imagination. It wasn't anything new or surprising to the locals though, as Indonesia lies on the Ring of Fire; a major area in the basin of the Pacific Ocean where many earthquakes and volcanic eruptions occur.

When we caught up with Sue and Dave for drinks we were discussing the earthquake. They were staying about 10 minutes' drive away from us and said they had certainly felt it that morning too. Sue said, "Dave was in the shower and got dressed mighty quickly to go outside and see what was going on. Everyone from our hotel was outside too. It was a bit of excitement for the start of our holiday."

Winning the Longboard – Manifestation Style

We stopped to have lunch in Peekaboo café-restaurant. It is a funky place with awesome food, cocktails, and great service. Whilst there, Rob spotted two surfboards behind the bar. They were being given away on Wednesday night. All you had to do was go to the restaurant between 7 pm-11 pm that coming

Wednesday and you'd get a raffle ticket for every drink you purchased. He was keen on the green longboard.

On Wednesday, we met Johnny and Georgia, friends of Ryan's – who had landed in Bali the day before – to catch up for a drink at 6 pm at Old Man's Restaurant. I saw their post on Facebook and messaged them. They too, had felt the earthquake and wondered if they were imagining it.

Rob had already said we needed to be at Peekaboo Café later as he was going to win the longboard. There was never a hesitation in his confidence that he was going to win it.

We got to Peekaboo, ordered dinner and drinks, and Rob started collecting the tickets. He had told the staff he was going to stay and win the longboard; the other patrons were bringing their tickets over when they left and wished him good luck.

It started getting embarrassing when he told a group of young surfers, "Don't worry mate, I got this," and they just looked at him and laughed.

Johnny and Georgia left, leaving their tickets with Rob. Not once did he hesitate and suggest going home. He was convinced he was going home with that green longboard. And... you guessed it, he won it!

The funny thing was though we had to buy a fin, strap, and cover for his new "free" board. He was rapt. He used it many times before we came home. It was huge though, and it looked funny on the side of the scooter. We nearly took out some pedestrians when turning corners riding to the beach. I've always been a fan of keeping a positive attitude, but now I am convinced that a positive attitude wins the day.

Jatiluwih Rice Terraces

We went out on the scooters with Sue and Dave, riding through the lush, brilliant green rice fields on our way to the Jatiluwih Rice Terraces. I had never heard of them.

The rice terraces are located in the middle of Bali near Ganung Batukaru, about two and a half hours' ride away. We stopped along the way to take in the views, take photos, and have a swing. The terraces comprise of over 600 hectares of rice fields following the flowing hillside structure of the Batukaru mountain range. It costs a small amount to enter the heritage site. As we rode in on our scooters, the scenery was breathtaking.

Jatiluwih is derived from two words; "jati" which means "real" and "luwih" which means "good" or "beautiful." And it really is.

We had lunch at one of the restaurants and then went walking through the rice terraces. There are several different tracks or trails you can take, but whichever one you choose, the landscape is beautiful. The terraces are cut into the side of the mountain to create flat plains with a basin to trap the water that trickles from one terrace to the next. It's so pretty up close, but breathtaking from a distance. It was such a great day.

On another day, we set off to Ubud on our scooters again. It's the only way to travel, if you're game. Believe me, it can be a bit scary at times. I don't know how Rob and Dave do it; you really need eyes in the back of your head when riding scooters in Asia. Sometimes, I purposefully look in the other direction, as it's often chaotic with cars and scooters all locked in small spaces, revving their engines, and waiting for the lights to change. The scooters are often up on the sidewalk to inch that bit further ahead. They're very impatient and that's when accidents occur. I can't imagine what tourists are thinking when they get on a scooter for the first time, especially when it's in Asia.

Back to Ubud; it's roughly an hour's ride from Canggu, depending on the traffic, of course. Bali's traffic is getting worse. It's consistently busy and often delayed due to traffic congestion. The infrastructure was never considered when the tourist population grew, I'm sure of it.

A.R.A.K. coffee shop is our favourite, so that was our first stop. It's a quaint little place with really good coffee and a clothing shop upstairs. Just near the coffee shop is the Campuhan Ridge Walk which is a very popular walk along the ridge in Ubud.

The track is a few kilometres long and edges its way through the rustic jungle surrounds towards restaurants, cafés, and accommodation. The views of the hills and green vegetation are beautiful, especially at sunset. It's purely a walking track (you can't get bikes up there), so we rode around the opposite way to get access to the restaurants and cafés. We stopped at Billy's Terrace café for traditional Balinese food, beer, and fresh coconuts, and admired the amazing view of the rice terraces and farm houses. Then we rode through Ubud on our way back to Canggu, stopping at Deus for my favourite happy hour bubbly, then headed home.

Snowing in Bali

Rob was reading *Snowing In Bali* when we were in Canggu. It's a compelling true crime story of the organised drug trafficking and dealing scene that's made Bali such a well-known destination in the global distribution of narcotics. Written by Kathryn Bonella, it's a true, inside account of the rise and fall of some of the drug Mafia world's biggest players. Seminyak and Canggu were among the central locations mentioned in the book. As Rob kept reading, we were fascinated by where things were, such as the locations of the "drug lord house" and beach clubs they mentioned. As we were in Canggu, for a bit of fun, we started exploring to see if we could find the said abandoned house of the main character in the book – which we think we did.

Then we were watching all the trendy young blokes in the beach clubs, trying to figure out which ones fitted the "drug lord" persona, according to the book. Plenty of them! It was all a bit of fun.

*****

On Wednesday 23rd July, they held Galungan celebrations for the Balinese Hindus. We were staying at Mikuk homestay in Canggu where Nuri, the owner, and her family were preparing offerings for their temples. It is a holiday in Bali and Nuri was explaining the purpose of the celebrations, which is to welcome the spirits of family, marking the time when the ancestral spirits visit the earth. The last day of the celebration is Kuningan, when they return. Along the street were many parades of dragon-type costumed men, demonstrating the

Holy Borong dance. They would stop and dance outside each house to welcome the good spirits with holy water and dispose of the bad spirits. It was very festive and vibrant.

We stood at the front of the homestay with Nuri and her extended family as she explained the meaning of the dance to us. Her mother had been making baskets from vines all morning to carry their offerings in, and then laid them at the foot of the temple and in the middle of the driveway.

The baskets were filled with some or all of the following: flowers, petals, food items, and money. Then a lit incense was laid on top. As they lay the offerings at the temples or on the ground, they said a prayer. As the parade came past, it stopped in front of each home and performed the dance to welcome the ancestral spirits and sprinkle holy water on the offerings. The families were very grateful as they watched the parade move up the street.

A few days later we headed back to Phuket via Singapore for another two weeks of our exercise regime of boxing and gym.

MY TOP TIPS FOR DINING OUT

1. Only drink bottled water or spring water if you're comfortable that it's not local water.

2. If you're not sure, only drink bottled drinks at bars and restaurants e.g. beer, Bacardi Breezers.

3. If you're not sure of the food, order fried food (such as spring rolls) as all the bacteria should be fried out of it.

4. Order their local fare – nasi goreng, fried rice – as it's usually good and safe for westerners.

5. Go to busy restaurants. It usually means the food is fresher as it's cooked more frequently.

6. A "little bit spicy" usually means it's "very" spicy for westerners.

7. Take a Yakult daily to protect your gut.

8. If you take probiotics, bring them with you as they're very expensive in most Asian countries.

9. If you feel like the food you've just eaten is "dodgy," take charcoal tablets to kill the bacteria.

10. Check out the reviews of restaurants if possible. Go to popular places.

HEALTH UPDATE – WEEK 28 – (July)

We were feeling great by the time our buddies joined us again. They definitely noticed the differences in us, both physically and emotionally.

We decided to relax the fitness regime a bit this month and enjoy cocktails, wine, and beer. We still made wise food choices but weren't concerned if we didn't do our daily workouts.

Weigh In:

Jenny – 64.5 kg   Lost 7 kg
Rob – 85 kg   Lost 22 kg

Exercise:

~ Walking 5-10km daily ~   ~ yoga ~   ~ meditation ~   ~ gym ~

Typical Daily Food Intake:

Breakfast: Muesli and fruit, eggs, coffee
Lunch: Nasi goreng, chicken and basil
Snack: Nuts and/or fresh fruit
Dinner: Prawns or chicken and vegetables
Drinks: Water, protein shakes, tea, and some alcohol

Chapter Nine

Boxing and Typhoons

> "Today is the only day. Yesterday is gone."
> – John Wooden

Boxing Camp #2 – Bangarang Gym

We booked our second boxing camp not long after the first one in May. We loved it so much, we thought we'd do ten nights at Bangarang Gym near Chiang Mai in Thailand.

We were definitely getting fit by now, so at first, the one-and-a-half-hour training sessions weren't as hard as we thought… or were they? Fatigue started kicking in at about day three. The trainers were awesome and fun but hardworking. Again, the warm ups were the killer. This gym had us doing circuits, including tyre flipping (which I hate), ball games, and generally exhausting exercises around the gym area. We both sustained injuries from the warm up team sports; we were always put in opposite teams and got quite competitive.

The other guests were great. We got along really well with them and still keep in touch. It was August and really wet. I think it rained most days. The staff, food, and environment were amazing. This camp is when we started to notice we were fitter and were looking much better. We had to buy Rob new clothes along the way, as he had lost so much weight. But here he was starting to really increase his fitness, strength, and stamina. He could have stayed longer and would next time. It's a new happy place for both of us.

Rob did a lot of boxing and was improving significantly during this camp. He could feel it and loved it. It was great to see him embrace something other than work. He was feeling more physically capable all the time. Another guest, Adrian, who had been competition boxing previously, was helpful by training and sparring with Rob in the ring.

The villas were separate and quite luxurious. The food (three meals per day) was healthy and delicious. The boxing classes here were 10:30 am-12 pm and 3:30 pm-5 pm. They were only one-and-a-half-hour sessions, but still exhausting. Spare time included: massages, bike riding through the rice fields, shopping in Chiang Mai, swimming, or resting. We didn't care to go out, nor did we have the energy. Netflix was installed on the TV so we binge-watched Peaky Blinders at night.

Peaky Blinders, for those of you that don't know, is a gangster family epic set in Birmingham, England in 1919. It centres on the Peaky Blinders gang and their ambitious and highly cunning boss Tommy Shelby. It's a bit bloodthirsty for me, but it's quite intriguing at the same time. Luckily for me, they had subtitles as their accent is really difficult to understand. I think we managed to watch three series in just ten nights!

We practiced yin yoga before bed to stretch and settle our muscles for the night. We did a little stretching after each boxing class, but I found that wasn't enough, especially doing so much exercise.

We were very fortunate to be there when three of Bangarang Gym members were in competition fights in Chiang Mai. All the guests, staff, and trainers went to the fight via minibus. We really felt like part of the family. It was a great atmosphere and awesome to be involved in a very local event. It was in a covered, outdoor arena near the night markets in Chiang Mai. It was pouring down rain for most of the night but this didn't seem to worry anyone. The tickets cost 500 baht (approximately AUD $24) per person and there were six fights. Bangarang's team won two of the three fights they were in.

After the event, we went with the group to a restaurant to celebrate with (another) meal and drinks, getting home around 2 am. What a treat!

*****

During the camp, we decided to have a rest day to break up the constant training. Monday was our elected day and we decided we would go into Chiang Mai, have some lunch, and a massage. We got a car into Chiang Mai and Noi, the driver, told us to catch a local bus (which is like an open-air ute with a roof on it) back to the camp as it would be so much cheaper. We hadn't really tried this before, mainly because English is not so common in the outskirts of cities. But we thought, what have we got to lose? Noi said, "Catch a red bus back to the station and a yellow bus back to Mae Rim. It should cost 100 baht to get back for both of you." That's a total of approximately AUD $5. She then gave us a note in Thai to give to the drivers to help us get back. It all went quite smoothly, and it took nearly an hour and a half instead of 30 minutes by car as the bus stopped at "all stations." It was an interesting and very local adventure, which we loved.

Elephant Sanctuary – Mae Rim, Thailand

We hadn't been feeling the need to support any elephant enterprise until we went to Chiang Mai. It was recommended because it is an ethical sanctuary with only five elephants in their keep. They had rescued them by paying for them to be released from "working," either as riding elephants, circus entertainment, or lugging logs.

We began the afternoon by changing into the provided clothes, which looked like the handlers' clothing. It was maybe a gimmick, but fun anyway. We walked around with the elephants and fed them bananas, plant matter, and prepared rice and vegetable balls – just part of the 100 tonnes they eat per day. We were given shoulder bags that held the sugar cane and bananas to feed the elephants. Their trunks are coarsely covered in prickly hairs and the snout is like an inquisitive periscope, looking for food. It's really weird feeding them.

Mostly, they just help themselves to food from your shoulder bag, which is quite funny. Their eyes are soulful with amazing eyelashes; quite a beautiful beast.

After feeding them, we went into the mud pond with them, and covered them with mud, which they seemed to appreciate. When they left, we were all floating around in the mud, which was quite a bizarre experience. The humans and elephants then parted ways, we hosed off the mud, and had happy hour in the pool.

Dinner was a traditional soup-style meal that was provided and we made ourselves, which was delicious.

It was a delightful day. Rob enjoyed himself so much more than he expected. Big tick.

Japan to See Ryan and Airi

Waiting for a flight at Bangkok airport, we stopped to have a nice glass of wine and a beer to celebrate our achievements thus far. It was a "smell the roses" moment; after all, we felt fabulous and were living our dream, currently on day #210.

We caught a flight (booked only a month ago) to Fukuoka airport in Japan. Ryan and Airi had moved there when Ryan got a new job in April. They had settled in now and were gracious enough to host us and show us around. Oita prefecture is about two hours' drive from Fukuoka city, on the south island of Kyushu. It's quite country-like in Nakatsu where Ryan lived.

Ryan and Airi met us at the airport and we spent some time with them before Airi went off to work, then we ventured around Fukuoka. It was really hot when we were there as it was during their summer. This was another reason why we went in August; to stay with the "endless summer" theme of our trip.

It was late afternoon and we thought we might stop for a drink and a snack. We found a quaint, quiet, old English pub in which we got quite comfortable. It's hilarious to watch Ryan converse in another language and order our drinks and food. We stayed for quite a while, catching up, laughing and telling stories of all of our travels. We then met Airi and went to dinner.

The next day we went for a drive around the countryside watching the beautiful, green landscape and enjoying Ryan and Airi's company. It was a really hot day to start with, until it started raining and got really windy. There were warnings that a typhoon was approaching. Typhoon Krosa was in town. It bought dangerous storm tides, heavy rainfall, and short flooding to areas of western Japan and Kyushu, where we were. We were out on what started as a beautiful sunny day and ended up wearing ponchos to protect us from the harsh rains. Sounds a little like Melbourne's weather.

We marvelled at the size of their tiny flats in Japan; Ryan and Rob needed to duck their heads to get in the doorways. Everything is compact and doesn't really cater for taller westerners. The kitchens are tiny too, just a sink, a burner or small oven, and some cupboards. Parking is extremely expensive in the city areas. Ryan has got a car but it was cheaper to catch the train.

On one of our day trips, Ryan and Airi took us to an onsen, which is a Japanese natural hot spring bath. They are plentiful, due to Japan's volcanic activity. When you drive along a mountainside you can see small steam puffs rising from the trees on the side of the mountain. These are onsens, where the steam was coming off the hot water. The prerequisites of an official onsen are that the water must contain at least one of the 19 designated chemical elements that naturally occur in hot spring water and it must be at least 25 degrees Celsius.

Onsens are usually communal, which doesn't necessarily appeal to westerners, but is a beloved part of Japanese culture. Oh, and you go naked. Tattoos are not permitted in many public onsens, so luckily we got a private one! Rob and I had our own little hut complete with shower, toilet, and onsen. This onsen was made of natural stone and was the size of a small pool or large spa. We had our private onsen for an hour. It was very relaxing.

We went to Fukuoka city for dinner and drinks. We stopped at a lovely restaurant on the Naka River to enjoy the beautiful view. We indulged in the best dumplings and sparkling wine. This restaurant had the toilets under the stairs which made the doorways and ceiling really low. I'm not sure how Rob and Ryan stood up in there. It's hilarious when they had to duck to enter doorways.

I love Japanese food; dumplings and okonomiyaki (vegetable pancakes) are my favourite. Rob likes the food but is not as big of a fan as I am. Ryan and Airi cooked us a meal of soup, meat, and noodles at their flat, which was delicious.

It was a great catch up. I had been missing him and the rest of the family. It was really interesting watching Ryan integrate into another culture so well.

We stayed with them for six nights and flew back to Phuket via Singapore and stayed at Patong Beach for another two weeks.

Phuket to Bali

We were back in Patong Beach to continue getting fit. Rob signed up for another month at Maximum Fitness gym and I got a two-week pass, as I was moving on to Bali in two weeks' time for a yoga teacher training course. We really loved the gym there; the staff were wonderful and they had yoga as well.

The women in the yoga session were lovely, but nobody really spoke English. I was the only westerner there. Most of the instruction was in Thai but I managed to keep up with the sequences. It was funny though, when we were doing an exercise that involved two groups counting down from one hundred. I got lost when they kept changing from Thai to English. It was hilarious, but I'm not sure how many repetitions we actually did in the end.

Rob and I got to know the trainers and many of the tourists that visited regularly. We could feel our strength increasing too. Some days we would stop at the food court at the local shopping centre, Jungceylon, for a local, cheap lunch.

Other days, we had lunch at our "regular" restaurant, close to our hotel. It was so small that they had three tables inside and

Boxing and Typhoons

it was usually just locals. We noticed they didn't give us a jug of water, which was good, as we probably couldn't stomach the local water. They got to know us and we ordered the same meals every time – usually basil chicken and rice for Rob and chicken fried rice for me. It cost us approximately AUD $5.70 or AUD $9.85 with two mango smoothies. The food was fresh and delicious and the family owners were really nice.

I remember when Rob came over to meet me in Bali. He had gotten sick on the last day in Thailand, and we thought it was from the water. He got a bit daring and drank the local water from the restaurant, which was not a good idea. He was so sick with stomach cramps that he had to go the doctor's clinic for treatment and medicine, which cost AUD $255. It took him many days to recover, he was so sick. It's easy to get complacent when you've been there so long and haven't been sick. Lesson learnt; he stuck to bottled water after that.

Just One Drink (lol)

In Phuket, Rob and I found this little bar called Mookies Bar. Mookies Bar was near where we were staying at the Aspery Hotel. It was just a nice little bar on a corner of the main road.

Now, the small bars in Patong Beach, if you've ever been there, are *tiny*. Mookies had eight bar stools to accommodate eight guests – that's it. But the impressive part is they had six bar girls. Six of them and the owner, for potentially eight customers. They had two bells; a big bell hanging from the ceiling, which is the bell you ring to shout the bar and a smaller bell that's handed around, just for the bar staff. We usually didn't get involved in any of this because our budget wouldn't allow it and we were only stopping for one quick drink on the way home after a budget meal of a chicken gyros for AUD $4.

My chosen drink this night was chilled white wine, which was probably out of a cask but tasted okay. It was cold and refreshing. Rob usually drank Sam Miguel Light in Thailand. There were three other men there when we arrived and one of them left. Four of us remained in this bar for around four hours. I call this story, "Just One Drink."

There's a photo in the middle of the book that shows what one drink probably doesn't look like, but the night was so much fun and unexpected. One of the customers bought the girls fresh flower leis to wear and they started wearing them around the top of their head like a halo. One of the girls gave me one as well.

We had music videos on the screen behind the bar and were dancing to old favourites like YMCA, Macarena, Living on a Prayer, Highway to Hell, and more. It was a brilliant night. The bell got rung a lot and it cost us probably a week's worth of our budget, just for drinks. You might be wondering how we had that much money on us that night, but we had just been to the ATM to top up for the rest of the week. That is called the "blown budget." However, the memories are priceless.

*****

Before we left, I remember telling friends that I would let my hair grow out to its natural colour (no, it's not grey!) and I would stop getting my nails done (SNS), just to give my hair and nails a break from consistently being chemically altered. It would also save a lot of money, because that "maintenance" was not in the budget.

It was going ok because I put my hair up in the heat anyway and my nails were growing really well. However, I was feeling a little too "natural" and decided to get my hair coloured and cut prior to going to Bali for the yoga teacher training. It was the same place I had my eyebrows micro-bladed a few months earlier, and they used the same foil procedure and products as home. It was great, but wasn't really any cheaper than at home at AUD $199. It blew the budget but I felt great!

MY TOP TIPS FOR LOCAL CUSTOMS

1. Get familiar with local rituals or customs to save embarrassment or unnecessary scrutiny. There is plenty of information online.

2. Discuss local customs with taxi drivers or locals. They love it and are very helpful.

3. Be respectful when visiting other cultures.

4. Clarify prices before you get in a taxi or use a cab with a meter.

5. Some countries or regions don't allow alcohol or other behaviours, so be sure to check before you mistakenly do the wrong thing.

6. Bartering is part of many Asian countries culture; they expect you to barter. Shops will announce "fixed price" if they don't barter.

7. Tipping is also a big part of the culture in many Asian countries. Tip what you are comfortable with.

HEALTH UPDATE – WEEK 28 (August)

Feeling fit and healthy. We could see and feel it.

Mentally, we were calm and happy as well. We were now trying any adventure that came our way. We had been climbing mountains earlier in Sri Lanka, boxing in Thailand in May, going to the gym with a personal trainer in June, and had just completed our second boxing camp. Bring it on!

This is exactly what we came away hoping to achieve.

Weigh In:

Jenny – 63.3 kg   Lost 8.2 kg
Rob – 83 kg   Lost 24 kg

Exercise:

~ Walking 5-10km daily ~   ~ yoga ~   ~ meditation ~
~ running ~   ~ boxing ~

Typical Daily Food Intake:

Breakfast: Muesli and fruit, eggs, coffee
Lunch: Gyoza, chicken and vegetables
Snack: Nuts and/or fresh fruit
Dinner: Japanese pancakes, gyoza, ramen
Drinks: Water, protein shakes, and tea

Chapter Ten

The Deepest Connection

"It is through gratitude for the present moment that the
spiritual dimension of life opens up."
– Eckhart Tolle

I left Rob in Patong while I flew to Bali. He had two more
weeks at the gym and boxing, then he would fly to Bali as he
didn't have an extended visa to stay in Thailand.

I had been looking for a 200-hour yoga teacher training course
for a while and never found one that clicked with me in content
or timeframes. I was looking for an intense program with a
duration of approximately 28 days. September was perfect, as
I wanted to do it later in the year to retain the knowledge for
when I got home to start teaching yoga.

I was still in touch with my yoga teacher at home, Claire, who suggested Embodied Flow. Tara Judelle is a well-known, highly regarded international yoga teacher and co-founder of Embodied Flow who happened to be taking a training course in September at the Yoga Barn. Perfect! After being accepted, I booked it. How exciting, I couldn't wait. I was nervous already, wondering if I'd keep up with the course. I needed to read some books prior to the course which I had ordered online and picked up from Ryan's home in Japan in August. Actually, he paid for them as a gift for me going on this journey.

I joined the course to become a yoga teacher, but I got so much more than that. This yoga teacher training was in Ubud, Bali, where I had been a number of times. I felt really comfortable there. I knew the homestay I would stay at, how far from the Yoga Barn it was, and felt confident staying there for a whole month on my own.

I am fairly social so the thought of engaging in a group for entire month wasn't too daunting. I was excited to meet a group of likeminded people, who, it turns out, were all younger than me. That was ok. I have adult children their age, so we got along well. We had an opening circle to introduce ourselves and our reason for attending this training. I spoke last and was quite emotional by the time I spoke. The energy in the room and people's reasons for coming were heartfelt.

The yoga teaching is great, but the journey was the most powerful part. I have been improving myself with self-awareness and healing for years now to overcome certain obstacles life had thrown at me, but I didn't realise I still suppressed some old emotions from years ago. It was enlightening and freeing to have so much time and support whilst digging deep to heal some very old wounds.

Every morning we had guided meditation and sat in silence afterward to reflect and journal. Tara is an insightful soul and her thought-provoking guided meditations were very enlightening. In fact, the idea and reality of this book and my future outlook on life came to light during this time. To have a mentor such as Tara is a rare find and I will be forever grateful for her support and wisdom.

We were encouraged to make our meditation seats comfortable as we could be sitting there for up to an hour sometimes. Much to our amusement, we all started converting our bolsters, blankets, and cushions into meditation "thrones," not only for comfort, but as our sacred space to internalise and find inner peace.

Following meditation was usually a vinyasa class with free movement. These classes were the formation of what was to follow in our journey. Free movement for body and mind is an amazing tool that fuels the soul.

I have been practising yoga consistently for about four years now and have realised the holistic benefits it holds for me. I will always benefit from the various techniques yoga offers, like meditation, breathing techniques, and the physical asanas. I am a better person for my yoga practises, on and off the mat (Rob would agree). The benefits I carry with me every day are self-awareness, personal boundaries, self-love, confidence, respect, steadiness, and ease. Being mindful and present is a gift for our continuous wellness.

On a health note though, my lung capacity and strength had improved significantly due to the breathing techniques I practised daily whilst doing yoga and meditation. I had previously suffered from bronchitis as my lung capacity wasn't great and I was vulnerable to getting chest infections and respiratory difficulties if I got sick. I haven't had any colds or bronchitis since taking up yoga. I love this added benefit.

Shine Your Light

For me, a lot of my focus and attention went into rediscovering my "light" that had been diffused a number of times in my life. But what I realised (again) was that it was me who was holding myself back; no one else has that power, unless I allow them. I already knew this, but during this intense time of meditation and self-reflection, it became more obvious to me and something shifted. I felt lighter and more confident. We all have our own "shining light" and should let it shine. I learnt a lot about myself, which I constantly embrace.

The food throughout our month was awesome. Every day for brunch, we were served a fresh and delicious banquet of salads, grains, lentils, vegetables, rice, and soup. We used so much energy while we were learning that the feast was always welcomed by the group. The days were really tiring, so by the time we left the yoga barn at 7 pm, there was only time for dinner, maybe a quick massage, and early bed. We were so focused on our days, the intense learning and self-discovery, that there wasn't really any time for partying or drinking. It was such a wonderful experience; I know it won't be the last immersion I participate in.

It turns out, I didn't need to worry about whether I could keep up with the course requirements. I just did. I was the oldest there, as usual, but never felt it. We all worked hard and achieved amazing things.

Lifelong Friends

During our trip, Rob and I made friends with locals and tourists. Some we keep in touch with regularly and some just occasionally, or only when we return to the place where they live. I have several homestay owners that have become friends, and they are genuinely lovely, caring people.

During the 28 days spent with the yoga group, we definitely bonded. There were four other Aussie women and I keep in touch with all of them, as well as others from the group. A bond is created when you spend 200 hours with likeminded people, and not many others would actually understand the personal growth you undergo in these circumstances.

Amongst these awesome people is Christie. Christie is such an amazing soul from Sydney, who apart from being fun and wise, is a friend for life who continuously compels me to do my best. We laughed, cried, sang, talked, danced in shops, drank cacao, and had way too many cocktails on occasion. We keep in touch regularly. It is through journeys like this that people arrive in your life for a reason. I am very thankful to have met Christie, Tara, and all of the others.

*****

I got very comfortable in Ubud. We got to know our favourite restaurants, beauty spas, and cafes. It was great to see others from the group nearly everywhere we went; they felt like family. On the full moon, many of us went to a Cacao Ceremony and Ecstatic Dance. This was something I had never attended before and was quite confronting for me. We all sat on bolsters, singing, chanting, and drinking cacao. Then we cleared the floor for dancing, which was a little crazy; just free-form movement that began with dancing on toes, then heels, and bent knees, all the while moving to the beat of the music.

It reminded me of some psychedelic 60s movie with weird music and LSD. I can't even begin to explain what happened during this dancing session; I'll just say that it was a weird experience that I probably don't need to repeat. Actually, in hindsight, it was hilarious. We all laughed about it on the way back, stopping at a quirky little wine bar and drinking cask wine. All in a night's entertainment in Ubud!

Rob was still staying in his favourite place, Patong Beach, continuing with his fitness commitment of gym and boxing. He took it quite seriously, going twice a day, eating well, hydrating, and having protein shakes, and was really pleased with his results.

He flew back to Canggu mid-September to surf. We left his longboard with Joe at the homestay. Rob stayed with Joe for two weeks. I was missing him, so he rode up to Ubud to see me on the last two Wednesday nights. It was our date night, so we would go to a lovely little restaurant I had found earlier in my stay and he would leave for Canggu in the morning. It was fun. He did this a few times which broke up the month.

MY TOP YOGA TIPS

1. I look online for what yoga studios are at my next destination. There are many in Bali, Sri Lanka, and India. I then look at reviews and usually check by going there myself and getting a "feel" for the studio and the teachers. You can also ask for recommendations from others.

2. Do a yoga retreat if you are really keen; they are life changing. Do your research or get recommendations first.

3. I take a "Manuka" yoga towel with me to lie on top of local yoga mats. It's perfect. It grips to yoga mats and gives me confidence of hygiene. I get it washed during the trip as well.

4. Try different styles of yoga, they're not necessarily the same as at home.

5. Different styles of classes and teachers make a big difference to your experience.

6. Check out timetables and costs online.

7. Try different local cultural ceremonies like a "water blessing," being blessed by a monk, or meditation at a temple. The experience will shift you.

8. Engage in a Kirtan celebration – devotional chanting, ecstatic dance, or a cacao celebration – which are all fascinating experiences.

9. Soak up the atmosphere as it will certainly be different to "home."

10. Remember, yoga is a practice for life.

HEALTH UPDATE – WEEK 38 (September)

I had been at yoga teacher training for a month and felt super fit, strong, flexible. I had stamina I hadn't had in years.

Rob was at boxing, gym, and kept trimming down whilst improving his definition, stamina, strength, and flexibility.

Motivation was easy. Our minds were relaxed and we felt confident and happy.

Weigh In:

Jenny – 61.5 kg   Lost 10 kg
Rob – 83 kg   Lost 24 kg

Exercise:

~ Walking 5-10km daily ~   ~ yoga ~   ~ meditation ~
~ gym and boxing ~   ~ surfing ~

Typical Daily Food Intake:

Breakfast: Muesli and fruit, eggs, coffee
Lunch: Nasi goreng, grains, and vegetables
Snack: Nuts and/or fresh fruit
Dinner: Prawns, fish, or chicken and vegetables
Drinks: Water, protein shakes, and ginger tea

The occasional chicken burger, cocktails and beer

Chapter Eleven

No Regrets, No Rabies

"Dreams become reality when we put our minds to it."
– Queen Latifah

Rob went surfing quite a bit during our last week while I was just happy to chill out, reading on the beach, and watching him. We were in Canggu for the last week and we had thought the whole way through the holiday that we might get tattoos to commemorate our trip, but we had let the thought slide.

It was on the third last day that we walked past the tattoo shop called The Tattoo Room in Canggu. I just wanted to get a mandala or something small on my ribs, where nobody necessarily sees it. Rob wasn't going to get a new tattoo now; maybe he'd just enhance an existing one with more colour. However, when he was asking the tattooist about that, the discussion suddenly morphed into him getting a tiger head on his upper thigh. Next thing I know, he's booked in for the next day to get it done and my mandala morphed into a palm tree that afternoon, which I'm very happy with.

Rob's tiger head tattoo took most of the day and into the evening. Nearing the end, he was getting irritated and it was becoming painful. At 9 pm we walked out of the tattoo shop to go home. We had two more days left and we were ready to head home by now. We had achieved everything we set out to do and more. We couldn't really go out in the seawater or in the sun with new tattoos anyway. We were ready to go home.

On our last days in Canggu, Rob was looking at a bulldog rescue page and found a beautiful tri-coloured Aussie bulldog, 12 months old, that we thought would be perfect for us. But to no avail; it was sold. So that was meant to be. I said, "We need to stop looking at dogs now. We'll just go home and see what happens."

We had no set plans for when we returned home at this stage. All we knew was that we were going back early because our granddaughter was due to arrive around early November and we couldn't wait to meet her.

I had my granddaughter's baby shower booked for when we returned home. Brittany had kindly kept the baby shower open until I got home, which I was grateful for. I felt like we had missed a lot of her pregnancy because we were away, even though we did FaceTime quite a bit. Nothing was going to stop me getting to the baby shower, which was on the first weekend of our return. It was a beautiful, fun day.

*****

Only a few days after we got home, I had a message from somebody wanting to know if we were still interested in taking on a bulldog. I wasn't sure how they knew, but didn't rule it out.

I rang to find out the details; Rossi was a six-year-old English bulldog, white and brindle, who had the most gorgeous face. I promised myself we would never get another white and brindle bulldog as our previous bulldogs were that colour and I didn't want to try and replace them. However, this woman contacted me to see if we would take him. Rob rang to discuss his suitability to us. We wondered, "Should we even take on another bulldog, as much as we love them, their life span is only eight to ten years." He really needed a good home and neither of us were working yet, so we thought we'd go and meet him on Wednesday. You guessed it, we brought him home with us. We call him Rosco.

He's a beautiful family addition with a lovely, energetic bulldog personality. We are happy to have him.

We were finished with our travels for now and needed some financial top-up. We were ready to come home and find our balance, finish our renovations, and spend more time with our family.

Integrating Back into Reality

Settling in at home was a little harder than I first anticipated, especially with the weather being unusually cold and wet. We were feeling the cold more than ever after spending so much time in the consistent heat.

Our Lessons Learned:

- **You can do whatever you put your mind to and enjoy the heck out of it.**

  We worked hard to get to this place of living our dream overseas and traveling for almost a year. We took notes, photos, journals, we blogged, we posted on socials. I soaked up the experience because all too soon it seemed like a dream, a memory. I'm getting to relive it by writing this book, which is an added bonus for me.

- **Listen to your intuition. You'll always be right.**

  Follow your heart, as my son, Ryan, says. We loved the experience and never once regretted a single dollar or a single second (well, wait, maybe breaking down in the middle of Sri Lanka with no phone reception or communication with the locals). But really that's just character building and creates stories to tell.

- **You don't need a lot to be happy.**

  After living with very little and in small spaces, we became less fond of the western ideal of owning a big house full of a lot of useless stuff, and more in favour of minimal living. We were more concerned than ever with our impact on the environment and the world after seeing so much of it and how others get by on so little. We are now much more content enjoying things like our veggie garden, a healthy way of being, our fur baby Rosco, and our quiet space near the beach. Our life has changed for the better. We live simply, happily, and love each other immensely. We will work to maintain a balance in our life from now on.

Our Relationship Now

"The best thing to hold onto in life is each other."
– Audrey Hepburn

"How's your relationship now?" is one of the most commonly asked questions we get, along with these others:

- How did you go being together 24/7 for almost a year?
- Is your relationship better or worse?
- How did you get along?
- How did you do it?

We have a really strong relationship anyway and we probably wouldn't have considered doing this if we didn't think things would be smooth sailing. So, I guess the compelling thing is to respect each other's space. We were living in a shared room most of the time, so we needed to be respectful of space. We constantly communicated about what we wanted to achieve.

We did have some time apart. I had the yoga retreat in India, the girl's week in Bali in April, and yoga teacher training in Bali in September. For most of those times, Rob flew over to Thailand to do some boxing and gym. He also indulged in his fun by playing pool at the bars with the locals.

The boxing camps were very bonding because we did the same thing with each other 24/7. We were learning new skills together. We understood the same exhaustion and we had empathy towards each other and our sore muscles.

At the second boxing camp, we got addicted to Peaky Blinders on Netflix. It wasn't really my thing, but we were both exhausted and it rained a lot, so it was nice to be able to enjoy it together.

We get along great; we can still have our own quiet time in the same space. I meditate, I read my books. Rob listens to music or watches YouTube videos on his phone. We have never used our phones so much in our lives; it is handy having mobile devices.

We still had date night. At Canggu, there is a beach band every night at the Batu Bolong Beach. We loved going there and sitting on the beanbags, watching the sunset, having cheap Bali beer and some dinner, and watching the world go by. People-watching is a favourite activity of ours, too.

Deus was another of our favourite cafés in Canggu. They customise and sell motorbikes and surfboards. They have bands there on certain nights and a nice happy hour at 5:30 pm. You can get two glasses of bubbly for AUD $10, which is like gold when you're over there, let me tell you.

We took the time to explore and the feeling of freedom we got to experience together was awesome. We had plenty of topics to discuss, from books we had read, movies watched, new adventures, and people we met.

I couldn't have chosen anyone better to share this experience with. Rob was open to new adventures and experiences like boxing camps, yoga, meditation, and Ayurveda. We discussed the whole idea extensively before we went but were certain we wouldn't have any regrets.

We went to get fit, which he embraced emphatically. But he was also open to relaxing, not stressing, and trying new things. Absolutely no regrets.

To answer the age-old question; we are probably closer now than when we left.

Reflection – Growth

When we got home, we couldn't believe we'd actually done this; from dreaming about it to living it one day at a time, one adventure at a time, and one discarded layer at a time.

The freedom is something that we had only longed for but never experienced.

Reflecting back on the whole adventure, I see we will never be the same again. Personal growth is abundant and appears in so many ways, including self-peace and self-belief. The love and respect for ourselves and each other has grown and we are confident in following our intuition again.

Missing the family was probably the only tough thing. Thankfully, technology allows consistent communication, especially visually. To see the kids and know they were happy and healthy meant the world to us and we could carry on with our adventure.

We felt totally relaxed, met new people, made lifelong friends, learnt to live in the moment, read books, learnt new skills, trusted in ourselves, lived in other cultures, and definitely found our adventurous spirits. We know now that we can still do anything we put our minds to. We have our health and happiness, and know that taking this time out to nurture ourselves was truly priceless.

We have left the hamster wheel well and truly behind. We are confident that we will find our balance, wherever that may be.

Transformation

When we set out in January, we were mentally and physically exhausted, depleted of energy, quite unfit, and unhealthy. We were both stressed from the past few years. We knew we wanted to change our lifestyle and get fit, but didn't have a set plan to put into action. We did most of it as we went.

To help us understand how to become fitter and healthier, we did research into:

- Which exercises would benefit us and how.
- What a healthy weight was for our heights, age, and gender.
- How to add some 30-day challenges into the mix/
- I enrolled and completed some online courses to learn new skills in social media, creative writing, etc.

- I held our own yin yoga classes in our room at night, particularly when we weren't sleeping well, or at the boxing camps, as our muscles got tight.

Mindset Changes

Along with our physical health, we vastly improved our mindset, and therefore, our mental health.

Things we noticed were:

- We stopped looking for alcoholic drinks to help us relax or unwind.
- Meditation slowed our minds and settled the stress, giving inner peace.
- We practiced gratitude daily, for our health, our current situation, our families, etc.
- Our confidence returned, with which comes happiness.
- Being present and dissolving day-to-day attachments is truly peaceful.
- Reading lots of books, some fiction for fun, but quite a few non-fiction books as well.
- Listening to music helped to relax us or inspire us when exercising.

We feel we have transformed in our whole beings; from our physical health, which shows, to our relaxed minds. During the trip, we worked on our health and mindset and were able to come back healthy, happy humans.

FINAL HEALTH UPDATE (October)

We definitely felt fitter and healthier.

By now, we had done two boxing camps, climbed mountains, surfed, lifted weights, and kept fit daily. We felt stronger and fitter than ever. I was still meditating daily for at least 15 minutes.

Rob was running daily and working out at the gym. He would find a gym in each new destination we went to and worked out daily.

We were walking 5-10 km most days, doing yoga, swimming, boxing, meditating, and Rob was running 5 km.

Our healthy eating was now just a daily habit. There was no snacking and little alcohol with lots of bottled water.

Weigh In:

Jenny – 61.5 kg   Total Loss = 10 kg
Rob – 82.4 kg   Total Loss = 24.6 kg

Exercise:

~ Walking 5-10km daily ~   ~ Yoga and meditation ~
~ Swimming and running ~   ~ Weights workout ~

Typical Daily Food Intake:

Breakfast: Muesli and fruit, noodles, omelette, coffee
Lunch: Chicken nasi goreng
Snack: Nuts and/or fresh fruit
Dinner: Prawn salad or chicken and vegetables
Drinks: Water, protein shakes, tea, and the occasional wine and beer

It's not all about the weight; it's about feeling healthy, happy, and alive.

We had no weight loss expectations; we just knew we weren't healthy and we needed to change. We know now this is how we are meant to be. We weighed ourselves when scales were available at the boxing camps or the gyms, and were usually pleasantly surprised at having lost more kilos, but we could already feel it from our loose clothing.

We felt lighter without looking at the scales and that was the aim.

Rob lost 24.6 kg, became fitter and stronger, made far healthier meal choices, strengthened his mind and body, became more flexible, and can now run and surf further than ever.

I lost 10 kg, became fitter and stronger, ate far healthier choices, strengthened mind and body, became more flexible, and can balance far better than previously. I am also now a qualified yoga instructor.

Many people have commented that we both look ten years younger.

We certainly feel it.

We would get a lot of comments on how happy and healthy we looked during the trip, and I usually commented, "This lifestyle suits us," or "Why wouldn't we look happy living our dream?" Looking back though, I also think we were shining from within, as we became happier, healthier, and more relaxed.

MISSION ACCOMPLISHED!

What's Up Next for Us

- To organise to travel every July for a month (once the chaos of the COVID-19 virus has settled)
- To complete writing this book and develop a Gap Year Planner and more
- Teach yoga and meditation
- Rob is continuing to stay fit and is now training for Tough Mudder later this year. He will make a team with Matt, Clayton, and perhaps Ryan.
- Spend time with family and friends – we did miss them all.

I'm very proud of what we have achieved in the last year; it truly is a transformation from exhausted middle-aged business people with depleted energy, to healthy, fit humans with a mindful attitude of staying this way. We certainly achieved our goals and will definitely do more extended trips in the future.

We believed enough to back ourselves, to venture out of our normal practice, and live what was merely a dream.

Rob is employed by a large cabinet joinery company, which is a different experience for him as he has been his own boss for nearly 30 years (and never had an interview or written a resume for that matter). It is very interesting and he is just enjoying the anomalies of having a job instead of running the whole business.

Three months in, and I'm still settling in slowly writing my first book – this book. I'm coaching women to be happy travellers and organising my first retreat in Thailand. Although as I write this, the world has been turned upside down with the coronavirus (COVID-19), so many are staying home at the moment. It's going to be a weird and interesting year, and we are so glad we took last year to have our Gap Year, as we wouldn't be able to travel as freely this year and the business would surely not have survived.

We are also completing our renovations amid the COVID-19 restrictions. Making the most of these unprecedented times.

We are now de-stressed from previous life events and feel confident and well-equipped to navigate through this unprecedented time in the world, with COVID-19 and related economic issues. We can't be thankful enough that we chose last year to take our Gap Year and live a little. Timing is everything.

We have continued with our health regime at home:

- Walking, stretching, and lifting weights daily
- Eating our evening meal by 7 pm
- No snacking
- Very little alcohol
- Drinking 2-3 litres of water
- Getting eight hours sleep per night

If you are ever dreaming of taking a complete break to find yourself and enjoy a new adventure, just listen to your instincts, and follow your heart. Remember that you are in charge of how and where you invest your energy.

Where focus goes, energy flows!

Good luck on finding your fun and freedom!

The Year That Was

"It's crazy what a year can do."
– Bianca Andresscu

So many people ask us how the trip went, especially because we didn't have much booked before we left. Did you do everything you set out to do? What was your favourite thing/place/adventure?

To answer, I think we did everything we wanted to do. It changed along the way, which was intentional; we did things we didn't think of before we left and we even stayed in one place for more than a month.

Therefore, the actual journey looked like this in the end:

Month	Location	Activity
January	Canggu, Bali	Self-care – relaxing and having fun (3 weeks)
February	Rishikesh, India	Yoga retreat (Jenny – 10 days)
	Patong Beach, Phuket, Thailand	Boxing and gym (Rob – 10 days)
	Canggu, Ubud, and Legian, Bali	Exploring Bali

March	Philip Island, Melbourne (home)	Reuniting with family and friends (1 week)
	Sri Lanka	Exploring and adventures
April	Canggu, Bali	Appreciating the beach
	Legian, Bali	Girls' week
	Canggu, Nusa Lembongan, and Ubud, Bali	Rhonda and Ian visit
May	Home	Family
	Byron Bay	Chilling at the beach
	Petchuban, Thailand	Muay Thai Boxing Camp
	Hua Hin, Thailand	Exploring
June	Patong Beach, Phuket, Thailand	Living
	Singapore	Checking out the architecture (3 nights to avoid visa)
July	Patong Beach and Kata Beach, Thailand	Keeping fit, visit with the Dare family
	Canggu, Bali	Hanging with Sue and Dave

August	Chiang Mai, Thailand	Muay Thai Boxing Camp
	Oita, Japan	Visiting family – Ryan and Airi
September	Ubud, Bali	Yoga teacher training (Jenny)
	Phuket, Thailand and Bali	Boxing and gym (Rob)
October	Canggu, Bali	Finish the trip where we began
November	Home	Reacclimatising
December	Home	Writing book (Jenny)
		Work / renovations (Rob)

Statistics

"It is the mark of a truly intelligent person to be moved by statistics."
– George Bernard Shaw (playwright)

When writing this book, I kept referencing my journal as I had kept so much information in there. I decided to put together some funny statistics. This following table is just for fun.

	KILOMETRES TRAVELED		SUNSCREEN
	1,194		600 mls
	AVERAGE TEMPERATURE		RAINY DAYS
	32°		27
	HOTELS STAYED IN		BOOKS READ
	41		R - 4.5 J - 18
	FLIGHTS		BEACH CHAIR HIRED
	34		22
	HOURS IN GYM		MEDITATION HOURS
	350		75
	BOXING HOURS		SUNSETS WATCHED
	65		136
	LITRES CONSUMED		YOGA CLASSES
	819		118
	SCOOTERS HIRED		Km's WALKED
	25		2730+
	POOLS USED		WEIGHT LOST
	39		27 kg - Rob 10 kg - Jenny

Top 10 General Takeaways

We are frequently asked what the top ten takeaways were for us. I have too many, so I have categorised them. I really could keep going, but maybe that's another whole book.

1. **The feeling of freedom (getting off the hamster wheel) and reducing responsibilities was amazing.**

   After being responsible for a business and family for the last 30 years, it was amazing to go away and feel that all we had to worry about was just the two of us. Where are we going to sleep? What are we going to eat and what are we doing for the day? Where are we going next? Nothing too complicated, just enough to be excited about every single day. It was amazing.

2. **Coming back more "ourselves."**

   We stripped back all those layers of stress and unhealthy habits, mentally and physically. By that I mean, we unwound our minds through relaxing, reading, meditating, exercise, and yoga. We also had time to just sit in the moment and be grateful; to not stress about the business, employees, clients, projects, renovating, etc. We didn't worry about anything, really.

3. **Living the reality of it – a surreal experience!**

   Every day was another day in paradise, another day for our endless summer, another day for #ouryearoff.

I wrote a journal every single day to catalogue what we did, what we ate, how far we walked, what the beach was like, and describing the areas we went to, just so that we would have it later. It was fun to relive the year again through writing this book.

4. **Discovering new places, new sights, new views, and new experiences.**

This was a bucket list on steroids really:
- Taj Mahal
- Muay Thai boxing camps
- Travelling in one country for a month
- Snorkelling with sharks and manta rays
- Visiting new countries
- Having friends join in on the fun.

5. **Getting fitter and healthier than ever was amazing.**

Our intention was to get fit and healthy. So, making choices to do so was easy. Eating better, snacking less, drinking more water and less alcohol all made a huge difference. Exercising daily and then increasing the intensity by challenging ourselves was really transforming.

6. **Completing challenges, physically and mentally.**

- Climbing mountains
- 200-hour yoga teacher training
- Muay Thai boxing camps
- Exploring on motorbikes and finding our way home again

7. **Healing emotionally.**

We were depleted of energy, physically and emotionally, from the last few years from:
- Grieving the loss of Rob's dad and supporting his mum who got sick
- Enduring stress from business responsibilities
- Making decisions and packing up the business
- Grieving the loss of our bulldogs
- Selling houses
- Moving and renovating

We were able to slowly process the emotions that were suppressed, heal our hearts, minds, and bodies. The beach, fresh air, warm weather, good food, yoga, exercise, and time all played a part in our healing. By the time we came home, we were in a much healthier place, emotionally and physically.

8. **Living simply – travel lightly.**

This was a great start to living the minimalist life! We loved the simplicity of living with just a small case or backpack for the entire time. The main benefit was that I couldn't purchase much as we had nowhere to put it, and I wasn't buying any more luggage (a first for me)!

9. **Listening to our intuitive selves to balance our life before it got too late.**

Winding down the business at that time in order to benefit ourselves was one of the best decisions we have ever made. To be self-aware enough to see the indicators of unhealthy "being" and to action it by listening to our inner selves was really a gift. It was a really hard last six months before we left – maybe because we could now see the end of this rocky road – but keeping our eye on the end goal got us through.

10. **Enjoying countries for longer periods.**

Spending more time in our favourite places like Patong Beach, Ubud, and Canggu was great. We could never go away for longer than two weeks whilst operating our own business, so it was very freeing to spend a month in one place, in one accommodation, and enjoying other cultures.

*****

Top 10 Moments or Experiences

1. India yoga retreat
2. Flying to Fukuoka, Japan to see Ryan and Airi
3. Taj Mahal
4. Swimming with manta rays at Nusa Penida
5. Snorkelling with sharks at Pigeon Island, Sri Lanka
6. Climbing Adam's Peak in Sri Lanka
7. 200-hour yoga teacher training in Ubud, Bali
8. Muay Thai boxing camps
9. Elephant sanctuary in Mae Rim, Thailand
10. Freedom Beach in Phuket, Thailand

*****

Top 10 Beaches

1. Freedom Beach, Thailand
2. Kata Beach, Thailand
3. Jungle Beach, Sri Lanka
4. Patong Beach, Thailand (awesome sunsets)
5. Canggu Beach, Bali (not for the sand, but awesome sunsets)
6. Byron Bay, Australia
7. Unawatuna Beach, Sri Lanka
8. Weligama, Sri Lanka
9. Arugam Bay, Sri Lanka
10. Nilaveli, Sri Lanka

*****

Top 10 Favourite Meals

1. Tuna Tartar – raw tuna on mango, cucumber, avocado
2. Nasi Goreng – Balinese fried rice
3. Okonomiyaki – Japanese vegetable pancake
4. Dumplings – pork and vegetable
5. Healthy breakfast – layers of yoghurt, muesli, and fruit
6. Pineapple Fried Rice – served in a pineapple
7. Chicken and cashew nuts
8. Crispy Duck – served with rice and vegetables
9. Banana and Nutella Pancakes
10. Masaman curry – vegetable curry

*****

Chapter Twelve

Don't Wait Till It's Too Late

"It takes as much energy to wish as it does to plan."
– Eleanor Roosevelt

Planning

Destination and Timelines

When we started planning this trip 15 months beforehand, we had many things to consider but we were already ahead of the game by knowing what we wanted to do. Traveling across South East Asia was our decision on destination, and maybe even living in two countries for six months each, for instance, Bali and Thailand.

That sounded like a dream to us. We had travelled to these destinations a lot over the last 12 or so years, so we knew we would love it. We were wildly excited to leave the chilly Melbourne weather for the whole of winter and create our own "endless summer" by going to these warmer climates. In doing this, we strategically decided when to visit other countries that do have cooler weather, like Japan. We waited for August to visit Ryan and Airi, as that was their summer, and it was really hot when we went. We also knew Asia would be lower-cost living that would suit our budget.

We decided that if we were going over to Asia, maybe we should do more than just two countries. There were other destinations we wanted to explore as well, like Sri Lanka and Japan. There was no definite itinerary as we wanted to kind of "drift" around to see where this adventure would take us. We wanted to have the freedom of choice as we went. Some destinations had given timelines, for instance, when our friends were coming to visit, or the girls' week in Bali, or to see Ryan and Airi. The rest was chosen along the way. It was great to be able to navigate around as we felt drawn to new places and adventures.

Every time we chose a new destination we needed to check if we required an entry visa, the application timeframe, and the cost.

We also had some timelines to consider, as I had four flights booked in already.

Dates we had locked in:

- February – Jenny's yoga retreat, India
- April – Jenny's girls' week, Bali

- March long weekend – home for one week
- May – home for birthdays

Things booked in along the way:

- Beginning April – Sarah and Mark, Sri Lanka
- End April – Rhonda and Ian, to explore Bali
- May and August – Boxing Camps in Thailand
- July School Holiday – Mark, Sarah, Phoebe, Elliot, and Naish, Phuket
- August (warmer weather) – visit Ryan and Airi in Japan
- September – yoga teacher training, Bali

We had friends coming over to experience "Jen's Tours," as I called them. I created and completed their itinerary, and all they had to do was get on the plane and land at the correct airport.

"Jen's Tours" included: an itinerary of destinations, accommodation, cost, where we would stay so that they could let their family know, budget required, visa requirements, and currency exchange rates. They were more than happy for me to take control – in fact, they insisted.

We weren't worried about organising the rest of the trip. That was the fun part, right? This was freedom; a "choose your own adventure." We had no idea what we wanted to do, apart from the initial three weeks. We thought we had an idea when we first set off to be chasing waterfalls and surfing. As it turned out, we only found four waterfalls, and not much surfing. There wasn't much surf at the time we were in Bali, Sri Lanka, or Thailand. Hence, why we ended up boxing.

Departure Date

After a lot of discussions around timelines for family and when to cease business operations and start to finalise equipment and storage, we knew that we would be able to leave Melbourne in early January 2019, for a year.

By November 2018, we knew for certain that we would be going, so I booked one-way flights to Bali for 8th January, 2019, which was surreal. I knew we needed to book onward or return flights prior to checking in to leave for Bali, but at that particular time, I was happy just to have booked a departure date as a "carrot" to look forward to.

We decided on 2019 because it was our window of opportunity, where our kids didn't need us and before our family expanded with grandchildren.

In discussions with others, it appears there are an array of reasons that hold people back. I'm not saying they're not crucial or real, but start considering where the "break" could occur, next year or after that. According to many people, the reason for not taking time out is having a mortgage, and people cannot foresee anything other than staying put to pay their mortgage off. Perhaps renting the house out to pay the mortgage or to pay for the trip, depending on your circumstances, is an option. We decided that we could redraw on our mortgage, if required.

People also say, "We'll go when…"

- "… the mortgage is paid."
- "… we have long service leave."

- "… this project is finished."
- "… the school fees are finished."

If you don't make a date, it will never happen. It is simple goal setting really, but if it isn't scheduled, it won't happen.

Another thing I hear a lot is, "We just need to get the kids through school, then it's our turn. I'll retire early." Well, this was what my parents thought. They'll retire and then they can do all the things they were saving to do, but they didn't get a chance. We don't know when our time is up. We really need to start taking this seriously, start living life now.

Budget

When planning, I started putting a budget together. We were researching accommodation whilst on previous holidays, to know what accommodation style and price would suit us over the term of the trip. We knew the approximate cost of living, accommodation, flights, and transfers, so I put a budget together, to consider for our savings goal.

There were also more financial areas to consider apart from the actual trip. For example:

- House bills/insurance/rates/amenities
- Rental income
- Mortgage repayments
- Car registration/insurance

Saving for the Trip

There are so many things in life we do out of habit that we really don't need to. We would consume one to two coffees each per work day. That's approximately $10 - $20 a day, that we could save if we had coffee at work.

While buying drive-through junk food is convenient, it can get expensive and unnecessary. We started organising lunches and snacks to take to work. Even though we needed to buy groceries to do this, it still worked out to be at least a saving of $5 each per day.

If it's important, you will structure your six or 12 months in planning to actually achieve this. You can:

- Cut out the coffees.
- Take your snacks and lunches with you.
- Don't buy Christmas and birthday presents; put that money away.
- If you don't have a mortgage, put an equal amount of money away. That will grow very quickly.

We did a quick calculation for 12 months of simple savings:

Activity	Amount	Savings
Coffee	1 coffee x 5 days a week = 260 coffees a year (520 for 2 people) 2 coffees x 5 days a week = 520 coffees a year (1,040 for 2 people)	At $5 per coffee: 1 coffee x 5 days a week = $1,300 ($2,600 for 2 people) 2 coffees x 5 days a week = $2,600 ($5,200 for 2 people)
Lunch	Packing lunch for 5 days a week x 2 people	Saving $5 per meal: $2,600 for 2 people per year
Presents	Christmas Birthdays x 2	At $250 per occasion: $1000
Mortgage	$250 per week	$13,000 per year
		Total: $19,200 - $21,800

Generally, our budget looked like this (AUD):

Accommodation	$35 per night
Food – 3 meals per day	$60 per day – 2 people
Entertainment	$20 per day – 2 people
Activities: gym, yoga	$20 per day – 2 people
Weekly spend	**$945**
Trip allowance (living expenses only, no flights etc.)	**$34,020**

This was quite tight though, but it made us think twice before spending unnecessarily.

We had other trips planned, booked, and paid for already, which were: the yoga retreat in India and the girls' week in Bali, which was taken into consideration. But clearly, we had a deficit so far and we hadn't booked any other flights, apart from the departing flights to Bali.

The most important one – and the most regularly used budget – was called the "blown" budget.

We pretty much blew every budget that we set.

However, in saying that, if you don't set a budget, you'll never know. We knew that if we really wanted to do something, this was the opportunity to do it. The budget was a guideline rather than an absolute.

We had spending money each day, which was amusing. It took me back to our early adulthood where you would budget so hard and give yourself $20 a week to spend.

Well, you know, I think we had $30 a day, which was hilarious. If we wanted to drink – and my preference was for white wine which cost AUD $10 for one glass – I would think carefully. Therefore, my choice would be between a yoga class or a glass of wine, pretty much. So sometimes I alternated between those (and that's how we cut down on drinking!)

The Business

We wanted a complete rest from being responsible for a business and employees. We very briefly considered engaging a manager, but knew we were not going to relax if we did. So, no manager.

We did try to sell the business but the timelines got too short, and we also realised we wanted to keep our options open. After all, Rob had worked his whole life to build this brand and reputation. It would have been easy enough to come back, resurrect it with a new showroom, and pick up the old client interest to continue on. I had already been working remotely, online, as an instructional designer, so I could continue my project work anywhere.

House

We weren't leasing our house out, but we did need to put many items into storage, to allow room for Matthew and Brittany to live there with their normal items. We have a large block of land, so we could easily put shipping containers on it to store any relevant items, like business equipment and household items.

Personal Safety and Immunisations

We had already registered with www.smartraveller.gov.au. They advise you of any travelling hazards or dangerous destinations if you register with them, which is highly recommended.

I checked with our doctor on what (if any) immunisations or boosters we would need. Going on an extended trip to Asia meant more exposure to the possibility of catching rabies from monkeys or dogs. As there are many dogs on the beaches, they are territorial and tend to fight. They can be in a frenzy and accidently bite you as you pass them or monkeys may feel like biting or scratching as they approach to steal your things, or check your bags for food. Either way, I didn't want to take the chance of catching rabies. Even with the vaccine, we would still need to come home to be hospitalised for treatment. Having the vaccine just gives you more time to get to a hospital. The vaccine was extremely expensive, around AUD $600 for both of us.

That said, we took all of the vaccines suggested by our doctor, as we were going for an extended stay.

Gut Health

In Asia, we maintain and protect our gut health by taking probiotics or drink one Yakult daily, which is readily available in Phuket and Bali. I take a bottle of probiotics with us as they are expensive in Asia. We find they are a valuable resource for staying well in Asia. Always hydrate with bottled water.

*****

Here are my quick top 12 considerations to prompt you with planning:

1. Timelines and Duration of Trip
- Does the timeframe fit in with family?
- Do you wait until the school fees are finished and the kids have left school?
- How long would be long enough?

2. House
- To lease out?
- Get house/pet-sitters in?
- Where to store your belongings, if necessary?

3. Career break/business
Options may be:
- Unpaid Leave
- Long Service Leave
- Negotiated leave
- Put business on hold or engage a manager

4. Budget
- Weekly spend
- Accommodation
- Flights
- Home bills
- Spending money
- Rental income
- Other income

5. Cars
- Sell or store them?
- Loan or lease them?

6. Storage
- Shipping containers
- Storage unit/s
- Garage

7. Departure date
- Sometimes it's easier to set the date and work back from that. If it's scheduled, it happens.

8. Destinations and Visas
- What weather would you prefer?
- What cultures do you prefer?
- Is it about discovering and exploring?
- What is it you want to see? Any bucket list items?
- Check if your destination country requires an entry visa. This should be checked at least 3 months before entry date.

9. Safety and Immunisations
- Register with: smartraveller.gov.au.
- Check with your doctor for what immunisations you may need. This should be done at least three months prior to leaving.

10. Flights, Luggage, and Travel Insurance
- If using carry-on luggage, only 100 ml liquids can be taken. Put all containers with liquids in zip lock bags.
- Consider cost of flight over length of flight. Which is more valuable: money or time?
- Travel insurance is cheaper for the whole duration of the trip. However, consider special cover if you ride scooters or do extreme activities.

11. Photos/Storage
- Camera/phone or both?
- Organise a cloud storage system, DropBox, or iCloud to store your documents and/or photos.

12. Money Travel Tips
- Get a fee-free travel card from your bank.
- Take a spare visa/debit card.
- Advise your bank you are going overseas and the timeframe, so they don't lock your card from use.
- Cash exchanges are usually better in your destination country than the airport.

PLANNING

ACTIONS TO TAKE

- Start planning your trip of a lifetime, now.

  I have created an extensive travel planning guide at: https://jennycook.life/AdultGapYear_ToolBox, which will help you start to plan your holiday.

- Research your possibilities. Start thinking and talking to people.

- Plant the "seed" to your partner or loved ones.

- Start saving. Just a little bit each week can make it all possible.

HEALTH TRANSFORMATION

ACTIONS TO TAKE

- Journal and track your daily exercise, and build on your exercise over time.

- Reflect on your old habits and journal your thoughts to undo old patterns.

- Track your food intake to help analyse any deficits in nutrients.

- Wear a Fitbit, as it really helps with motivation. It gauges your steps and kilometres and helps keep you on track. If it's raining, change to a different activity or wait until you can get out and walk.

- Hydrate with water and electrolytes if it's really hot.

- Stop snacking.

- Challenge yourself and boost your confidence.

- Download free 30-day challenge apps – for abs or yoga.

- Download my top ten self-care rituals at https://jennycook.life/AdultGapYear_ToolBox.

Appendix A

Rhonda and Ian – Bali Itinerary with "Jen's Tours"

Date	Place	Accomodation	Cost AUD
29/4 – 2/5	**Canggu**	**Ecosfera**	**$356 including breakfast**
Monday 29th April Tuesday 30th April Wednesday 1st May Thursday 2nd May Friday 3rd May	Settle in with drinks at Ecosfera. Walk to La Brisa and beach. Dinner at Ecosfera. Walk to Finns. B/fast. Relax by pool. Boys hire scooters and explore. Dinner at beach near Old Mans. Walk to Finns. B/fast. Ride bikes to Tanah Lot Temple. Lunch and drinks by pool. Batu Bolong Beach, watch band – pre-dinner drinks. Dinner at Tropikale café. 8 am Hatha Yoga. Swim. B/fast. Explore on scooters. Lunch at Deus café/chill by pool. Drinks at La Brisa (boat place). Dinner at Tropikale. Early b/fast. Walk and surfing. Check out 12 pm. Drive to Ubud (1 hr by car)	Boutique hotel with pool. Awesome b/fast included. 100 m to beach.	Booked, not paid. 4 nights at $89 = $356 Pay on arrival. Bike hire $7 p/day. Bring international licence. $25 for car – booked.

Date	Place	Accomodation	Cost AUD
3/5 – 6/5	**Ubud**	**Merthayasa homestay**	**$120 for 3 nights including breakfast**
Friday 3rd May Saturday 4th May Sunday 5th May	Check in at Merthayasa 2 Bungalow homestay. Explore/markets/chill by pool. Scooters – Tegenungan Waterfall. Anumana restaurant for lunch. Pool – swim. Dinner – Café Lotus. Bikes to Sumampan Waterfall. Local lunch. Relax. Dinner at Ibu Susu Japanese restaurant. Try the cocktails!	Double room with ensuite within a Bali home environment. Basic breakfast incl. Can walk to markets.	Fast boat to Lembongan $45 return each. Booked not paid.
5/5 – 9/5	**Nusa Lembongan**	**Dream Beach huts**	**$312 for 3 nights including breakfast**
Monday 6th May Tuesday 7th May Wednesday 8th May Thursday 9th May	Check out from homestay. 9 am shuttle to Sanur. Fast boat to Nusa Lembongan. Arrive by 11.30am. Lunch at Dream Beach Huts restaurant. Swim. Snorkelling at Manta Ray Point and Crystal Bay. Lunch and dinner at resort. Check out Devils Tear Drop – blow holes. Explore/chill? – check out 2 pm. Fast boat back to mainland – head to Sanur for a drink and walk. Car to pick us up for the airport. Flight 11.15pm	Basic thatched huts facing beach with infinity pool. Basic b/fast included. Awesome sunsets. Car organised from Merthayasa He will have our luggage.	Booked. Pay on arrival. Airport drinks at 9 pm.

DISCLAIMER - All activities are suggestions only and itinerary can change at any time!

Afterword

I'm so pleased you read this book and I hope you have gained some inspiration and insights from our experience to embark on your own Gap Year adventure – because, really, life is so short.

It can seem like a tricky process initially but it's just a process of working through the logistics. So, if you read the whole book without doing the action exercises or downloading the templates, take this opportunity to go back over the chapters and do the exercises; they are a handy tool, especially if you don't know quite where to start.

Am I saying it's easy? It can be.
Does it take planning? Definitely.
Is it worth it? Absolutely!

I wish you all the very best in your endeavours and adventures this one life has got to offer. Even if you just start out with a small experience you have wanted for a long time, you can achieve it just by visualising, planning, and doing!

If you want to find out more about my Adventure and Accountability Coaching program, and our retreats and events head to my website at: https://jennycook.life.

I have developed the Adult Gap Year Tool Box, which has templates and hints and information to help you plan your Adult Gap Year: https://jennycook.life/AdultGapYear_ToolBox.

Plan it. Do it. Love it. Repeat.
Enjoy life!

Love,
Jen xx

About The Author

Jenny Cook is an artist, businesswoman, educator, instructional designer, mentor, facilitator, yoga teacher, author, world traveller, and lifelong learner.

She is also a wife, a mother, a grandmother, and a bulldog owner.

Typical of her attempt to cram as much into life as possible, Jenny has many qualifications, including an MBA, Graduate Certificate in Management and Leadership, Diploma in Training and Assessment, Diploma in Visual Arts, NLP practitioner certification, Hatha Yoga Teacher, and Certificate IV in TESOL.

Despite all the labels, Jenny is really very difficult to put in a box. And if you tried, her enthusiasm, Energizer bunny energy, and zest for life would see her attempt to jump over it or stand on her head and flatten it.

Before moving to the beach a couple of years ago, Jenny was born and raised in Melbourne, the only daughter of Evelyn and Edward Solomon. Poignantly, Jenny attributes the early loss of both her parents to her zeal to live life while you have it!

So, it was no surprise to many when, after raising a family, moving seaside, and renovating their dream home, Jenny and her husband Rob "pulled the plug" on the normal rat-race of life.

They packed up and set out on a year of travel in search of the freedom to recharge and regain their lives.

In embarking on the trip, Jenny was being Jenny – designing her life her way, ticking off her bucket list of dreams, and hoping to inspire others to follow her lead and find their highest self through adventure.

That's what an Adult Gap Year is all about.

Acknowledgments

To my husband, Rob, for his unwavering love, support, and belief in me. This book wouldn't exist without you coming on this journey with me in the first place. You make my life a breeze and you support any "whacky" idea I have, allowing me to be me and live my life to the fullest. (And no, you're not retired!)

To my family, Matthew, Brittany, Isla, Ryan, Airi, Hailey, and Clayton. You will have this memory in your house for the rest of time! Thanks for your continued encouragement and support.

Thank you to all of our friends that travelled over to join in on the fun and contributed to the stories in this book.

To Sarah, who I saw three times throughout the trip, it was always fun to spend time and bubbles with you. Mark and Sarah, what fun and challenges we had in Sri Lanka and

Phuket – times we will talk and laugh about for years. Phoebe, Naish, and Elliott, I'm so glad you all came to explore one of our favourite places, Patong Beach, with us.

To my girls, Chrissy, Suez, and Jan, thank you so much for the great, much-needed girly time, bubbles, shopping and laughs. Can't wait for the next one!

To Rhonda and Ian, thanks for believing in "Jen's Tours" and enjoying the itinerary and adventures; exploring on scooters, cocktails, diving lessons with Rhonda. The fun and memories we built are priceless.

To Sue and Dave, who we meet often, but this trip to Canggu was so much fun, exploring, seeing new places, having laughs, and great coffee. Thanks guys! It won't be the last.

To Johnny and Georgia, although unplanned, it was great to have a catch up at Old Man's for a "cocktail experience" we won't forget.

To Tara Judelle and the Embodied Flow team, for the whole month of September, especially the 28 mornings of meditation and honest, embodied flow training. It has me seeing myself differently, believing in myself more, and allowing my "light to shine." I now really believe I'm funny, because of all of you! Thank you. I sat upon my meditation "throne" every morning with 20 others and grew personally, more than I expected.

To Christie, who keeps me laughing and supported me endlessly with this book, thank you.

Acknowledgments

Whilst we were away on our Gap Year, I was blogging, journaling, and taking photos as I already knew I wanted to write a book about it, but had absolutely no idea where to start. When we returned home, I registered for a workshop with Natasa Denman and Ultimate 48-Hour Author. Nat was so inspiring; I knew immediately I wanted to join in on the publishing fun with them. I signed up for the Ultimate 48 Hour Writers Retreat in February and have now written my (first) book. The Ultimate 48 Hour Author team of Nat, Stu, and Vivienne, guide and nurture first-time authors to write and publish their books. I've loved the experience and would highly recommend working with Ultimate 48 Hour Author, if you want to write your book into reality.

To all of my friends and family who have supported me along the way, most of you are never surprised with the "brilliant" ideas I have and encourage me endlessly.

To my Chrissy, who hears my endless list of "brilliant ideas" and is my "happy hour" confidant, even throughout the trip.

To everyone who purchased my book including at the pre-launch – thanks for having the confidence in me. And last but not least, to those of you who read some chapters to review this book – Karen, Sarah, Di, Christie, Ryan, Sonia, and Tania – thanks so much.

Thank you!

Notes

_____

_____

_____

_____

_____

_____

_____

_____

_____

_____

_____

_____